CHAPTER 1

BASIC PRINCIPLES AND GENERAL RULES

Most books of this type open with a brief history of locks; what the Romans did, the Chubb lever lock, who invented the Yale lock (three guesses), and so on. If you are up for that, and it can be interesting, try the *Encyclopedia Brittanica* for a good article on lock history, or any other encyclopedia of reference quality. One thing that never fails to amuse me is the Renaissance lock that shoots bullets or throws spring-loaded knives at anyone trying to bypass it with a pick. Instead of loading the book with easily accessible information, let's progress to learning a bypass technique instantly.

Consider the railing or partition latch that is installed

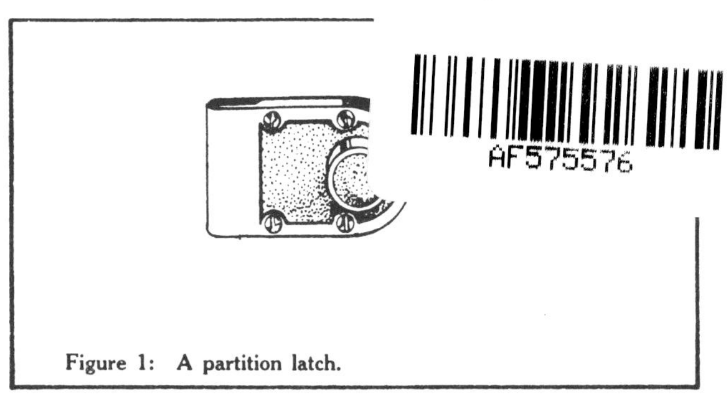
AF575576

Figure 1: A partition latch.

on the inside of most railings in banks, offices, courtrooms, and similar locations to prevent easy access via a swinging door. Irate customers who want to gain access *NOW* usually find the lock casing and start to jerk on the small brass knob that is mounted perpendicular to the case, but it doesn't get them anywhere. The knob is just a blind, the real latch-releasing mechanism is a false bottom that is pushed up with the finger tip. Notice here that the "key" was really only a little bit of knowledge on how the mechanism was put together, and the "tools" for opening were merely fingers. *The universal key to any lock is knowledge* -- understanding how the lock operates. Tools are only aids in manipulating the mechanism.

That is general rule number one: there are no automatic lock picks, only tools and skills. General rule number two: don't become keyway oriented to the point of single-mindedness. I have witnessed specialists actually attempt to pick a lock with keyway tools before even checking to see if the lock is actually locked, or worse yet, try to bypass a difficult lock and ignore the window locked with only a single latch that is easily bypassed. Always follow the path of least resistance. A good example of this is the guy who hides behind a drywall and stud wall during a gunfight, and is shot right through the wall by some guy who says "why not"? A BLT may attack actual lock tumblers, or it may attack the latching mechanism, or even the surface that the lock is mounted to or locks to. Furthermore a BLT may attack another link in the security perimeter entirely, and achieve the same goal. Always choose the path of least resistance.

Now let's look at four more rules of BLT, these rules apply to practicing.

#1, Know the lock mechanism perfectly.
#2, Never give up on a practice lock opening.
#3, When all else fails, cheat!
#4, Practice on the most difficult BLT and/or lock.

These rules require some explanation. If you are attempting a BLT on what you think is a simple warded lock, but actually is a two-lever tumbler lock, you will get nowhere fast. This is why knowledge of the lock mechanism is essential. Feeling different parts than you should be feeling with your pick is an immediate tip-off that while the keyway looks like a warded design, the internal mechanism is not. As for never giving up, remember that taking a five minute break is permitted, and often good for avoiding frustration, but the point is to never give up completely, because if you leave the lock locked you will probably not return for a second try. Cheating means that if you are completely baffled it is okay to open up a practice lock, or glance at the key bitting, or even checking to make sure the lock rotates in the direction you think it does. After such a pause, however, go back and again try to bypass the lock based on the new information. The secret is to never give up. Nothing is more impressive than popping open a disc lock in ten seconds, but you won't learn to do high security cylinders by opening disc locks, so practice on the locks that give you the hardest time. These rules may seem hard to follow at first, but eventually they will actually be a help to you in developing reliable techniques.

CHAPTER 2
WARDED LOCKS

Now that the groundwork is out of the way, let's start on the easiest type of lock. In *warded locks* the key, when inserted and turned, merely engages a locking bolt mounted in the case and slides it to the locked or unlocked position. In addition, the key may also lift or disengage a bolt retaining lever or spring;

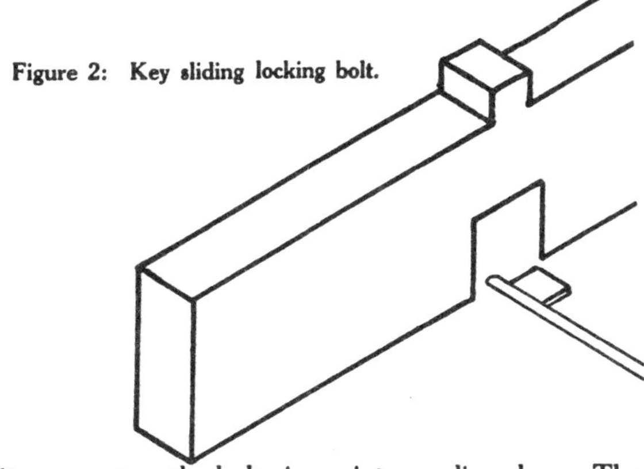

Figure 2: Key sliding locking bolt.

or it may act on the bolt via an intermediary lever. The spring prevents someone from using inertia on the entire lock assembly to retract the bolt, although this is still possible with some types of padlocks, (see rapping) and the intermediary lever serves to isolate the locking bolt from the key, but hardly adds to security. In fact, security here is at a bare minimum since any similarly shaped object will operate the lock (and all others of that type) easily. The next step up comes when the lockmaker inserts fingers or teeth of steel, called "wards", into the insertion path or the turning path of the keybit. A simple example is to cut the keyway with a tooth extending halfway into the keyway to block access. The lockmaker then cuts notches in the old key at the point where the ward would block the key, and so the key now passes the ward and enters the lock. Early attempts at warding concentrated on oddly shaped keyways cut into the lock covering plate, and keys shaped to to match. Later on, wards were installed to block rotation of the key within the lock case, and eventually a complex system of wards developed that required a key that was very

Figure 3: Keyway with matching cut in key.

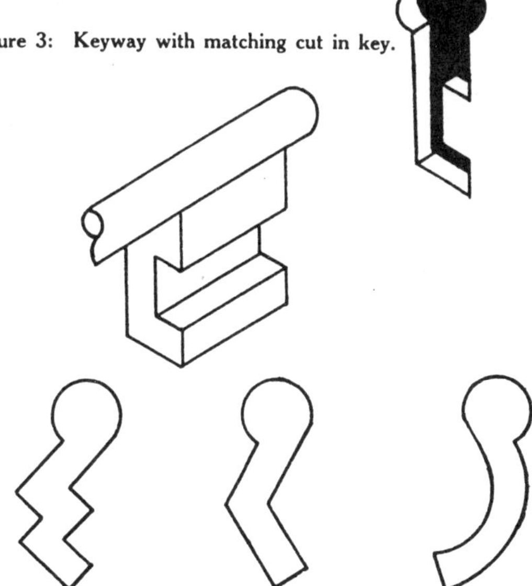

Figure 4: Different keyway shapes.

large, but cut to pass the intricate wards. Usually in constructing a lock like this the lockmaker would assemble the warding first, and then hold the key, which was pre-formed to a rough outline, in the center of a candle flame, coating it with soot. As the blade of the key was inserted and turned, the wards would rub away the soot and leave shiny marks where they contacted the key. The lockmaker would then remove the key and file it at those points so as to pass the wards. The next step was to re-coat the key and re-insert it in the lock for another attempt at turning. Eventually the point was reached where all of the key that obstructed turning was removed, and

Figure 5: Warding in key rotation path.

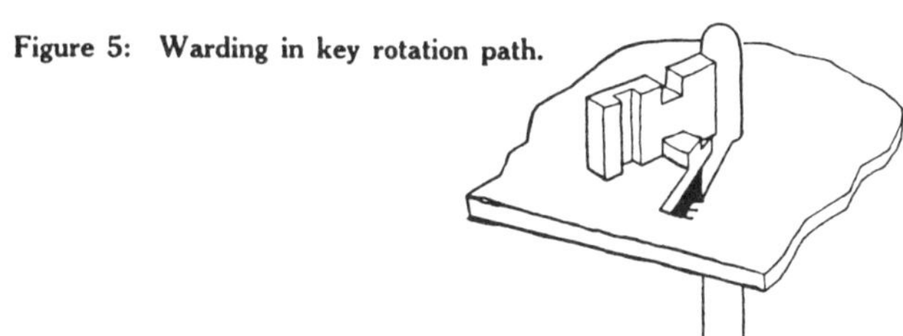

the key would unlock the lock. Duplicate keys of the day were fitted in the same fashion. It was assumed that the lockmaker did not also file away the key at those points where the bolt contacted the key, because if he/she did then the bolt would not be touched by the key as it rotated, and wouldn't unlock the bolt. Although increasing the number and spacing of wards increased the security of the warded lock slightly, anybody with a meager amount of skill could also smoke, insert, and cut a key blank to fit the lock, even without access to the lock mechanism, so therefore security was nil. As lock specialists of the day cut more away from their keys, eventually a point was reached where any more warding cuts in the key would have weakened it too much, hence the term skeleton key or a key

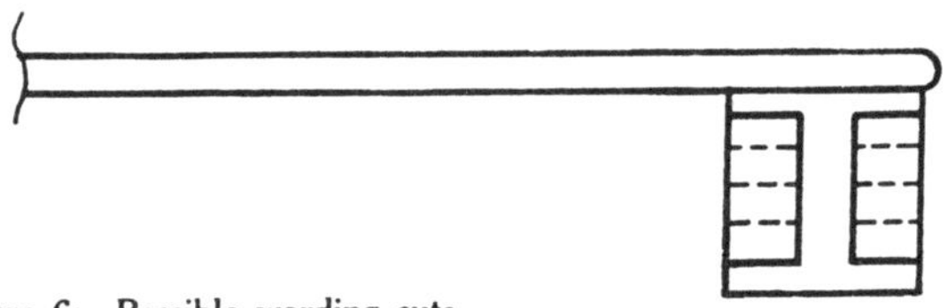

Figure 6: Possible warding cuts.

cut to the bare bones. Lock specialists of the day also found that a skeleton key for one set of locks with their attendant warding cuts, would also work well on other sets of locks, and the skeleton key eventually became an "L" shaped tool with a sturdy handle.

Common applications of the warded lock are many. Most locks characterized by knob and keyway both mounted on a stamped steel escutcheon are warded locks. These are very common in older 1910-1940 homes, and the strongest identifying characteristic is keyway profile. Care is advised, however, because many one and two tumbler locks are identical in external appearance to this type of lock. Chest and cabinet locks with keyway shapes similar to the above are also found on many applications. Frequently the keyway will have a post mounted in the top half of the keyway, and a matching hole cut into the end of the key so that the keybit is guided during rotation. Note that these posts limit keyway access a little, and they are called barrel or pipe keys.

Luggage and attache cases, diary, and hope chest locks are also usually warded. These may be old applications, some of

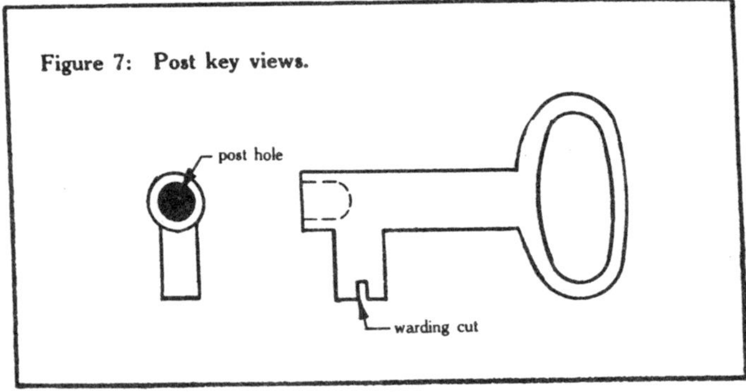

Figure 7: Post key views.

them having a rotating core that the key is inserted into which turns as the key does and limits access. The appearance of these locks is again often identical to lever tumbler locks, so look closely. Often a glance at the key, if available, may tell the difference.

Many different brands of padlocks, notably MASTER and SLAYMAKER bottom of the line models, are also warded locks. These feature laminated steel cases, and free spinning cores. If the core can be rotated by inserting a straight tool it is a warded lock; if not, it is a disc or pin tumbler.

Typical Key Profiles

Note the various kinds of warding cut in each key, both on the edges and the sides of the key blade. A glance at any pin or disc tumbler key will show that each still uses the warding principle in the form of grooves cut in the sides of the key. This increases the specificity of the key and limits keyway access to lock tumblers. The true warded key, however, shows no cuts of different heights. Be careful to distinguish between the square but different depth cuts of a lever tumbler key, and the square even depth cuts on a warded key. SCHLAGE Lock Company also markets a type of lock called a wafer tumbler whose keys have either single depth cuts in tumbler positions or no cuts, but a little keyway recognition practice will make these easy to distinguish. As the discussion progresses into the different types of lock, a lot of the foregoing will become clear.

BLT

Start your bypass training on warded locks since these are the lowest security and therefore easiest to work. The problem has two parts: avoiding all the wards; and contacting the bolt

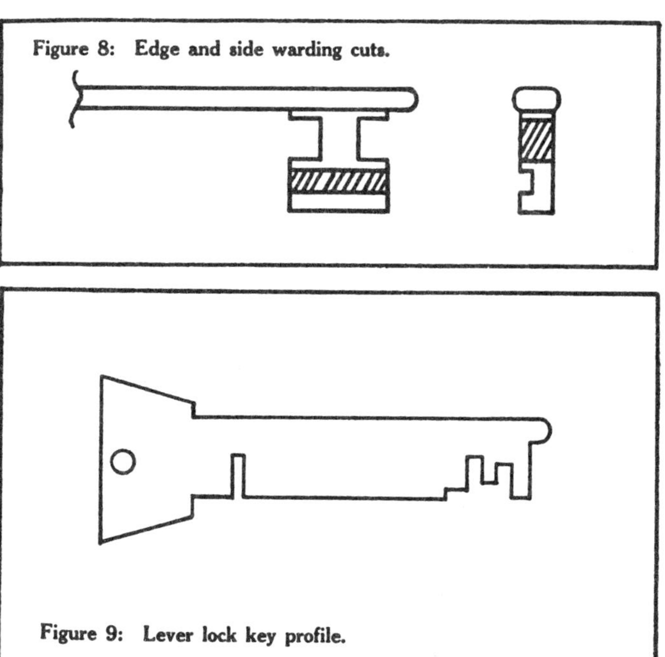

Figure 8: Edge and side warding cuts.

Figure 9: Lever lock key profile.

with a tool of sufficient strength and swing as to manipulate the bolt. For most mortise locks, a set of four or five different profiles of skeleton keys should prove adequate, and easier to buy than make. For good flexibility include two "L" shaped tools with handles. An alternate approach is to purchase several warded lock key blanks and use the soot/insert/file method, which we will call ward impressioning, to fit a key to a specific lock. Obviously the problem occurs when you attempt to use that key to work a lock with different ward combinations. Cutting the same key to pass a new set of wards may well weaken it, or even worse, the key may not be sized right to contact the locking bolt in the first place.

Note here that most warded locks are very rusty, dirty or stiff springed, so a strong tool with good bolt contact is needed. If the stock type of skeleton key does not work, a suitable blank must be ward impressioned, and that for every new lock. If you are using a skeleton key, try to select the key that has the least cut away from it, yet will still pass all the wards, ensuring that enough key will contact the boltwork. Now is the time to learn

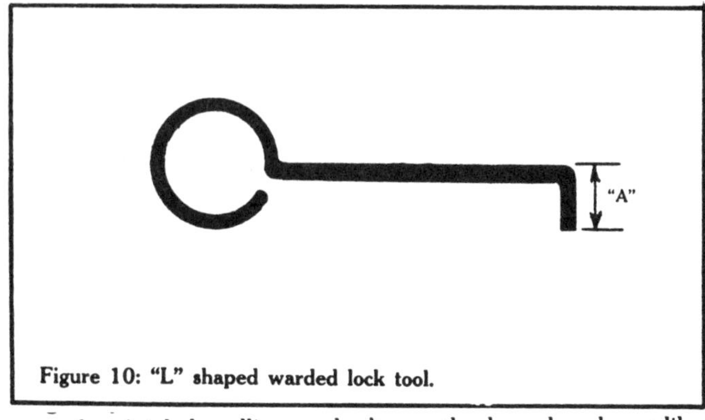

Figure 10: "L" shaped warded lock tool.

proper key/pick handling -- don't use the key slam-bang like you would on your old reliable house lock. Insert it slowly, feeling for obstructions until it bottoms, then turn slowly and feel for the notch cut into the locking bolt that the key blade must contact. A solid stop may mean you have encountered a ward. A more springy resistance will indicate the presence of a bolt retaining spring that also must be lifted. Because of this, two tools may be required, one to lift the retainer spring and the other to move the bolt. The best technique then is to disassemble the lock and make tools to fit before you go into the field. If you are in front of a huge iron door on a windy night with an armed squad looking for you, then you haven't done your homework. Prepare for such locks because they will stop you cold without the proper tools, even if they are rarely encountered.

Going back to the skeletons, take care when moving from a larger to a smaller key, or you may select one that is physically unable to reach the boltwork. Often the warded impressioning method can tell you where a bolt may or may not be, without filing. Consider modifying one of the stock skeleton keys only in a case of desperation, or try one of the "L" shaped tools. When making this "L" tool, remember to leave dimension "A" 1/16″ longer than the total height of your highest skeleton key. This is the shank to key bottom measurement. If you notice the tool is consistently too large, grind the end shorter, but remember that you can insert the end on an angle and so a little length is affordable. Pipe or barrel keys present a special problem of keyway access. One answer is to purchase several pipe type key blanks and then field modify them as necessary.

A step-type of tool, with a shank small enough to be inserted between lock keyway and post is shown in figure 11. Such a tool can easily bypass the pin in the keyway and contact the boltwork. Rarely is such a lock encountered.

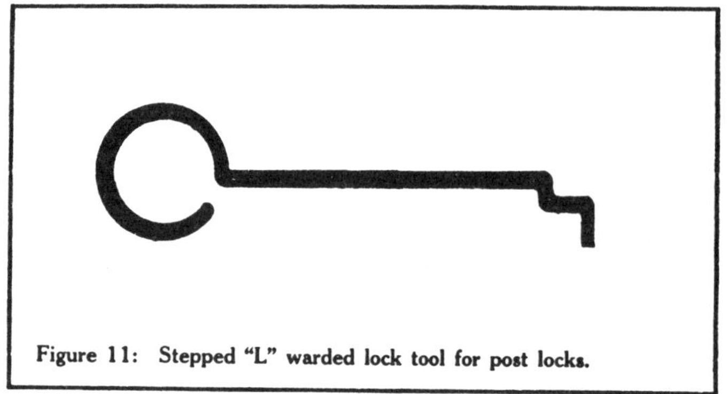

Figure 11: Stepped "L" warded lock tool for post locks.

Warded padlocks are very common, and here the best learning tool is to buy one of each make, impression the key that fits the lock to see where the boltwork and the key meet, and then cut away all other non-essential key material. By impressioning before cutting you don't cut away the bolt activating part of the key. Do not cut away the parts marked as in the regular impression system, but instead those parts that seem to be non-essential and marked. Use a little common sense here, and especially take care when inserting the key so as not to accidentally rub off some of the soot on the lock case, which would create a false impression. Also note that many of these locks have two sets of spring shackles that hold the lock shackle closed, so two sets of marks will appear, usually at the tip of the key, during impressioning. If you prefer to cut tools out of feeler or flat ground stock for these locks, coat the rough cut blank with soot, insert and attempt to turn, and begin to file away material from the key starting at the bow. Assume that there are two sets of shackles leaving marks, and if you complete all the other cuts, and the key will still not turn, then file at the set of marks farthest from the tip of the key. Often you will end up with a single bitted tool resembling a "T", which can also be used to open double shackle padlocks if the shank is long enough.

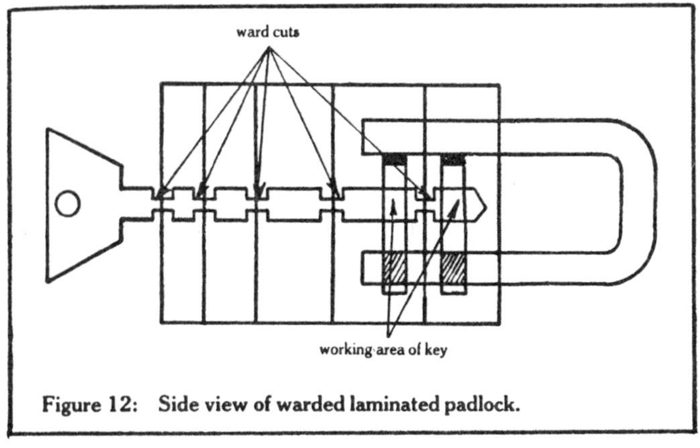

Figure 12: Side view of warded laminated padlock.

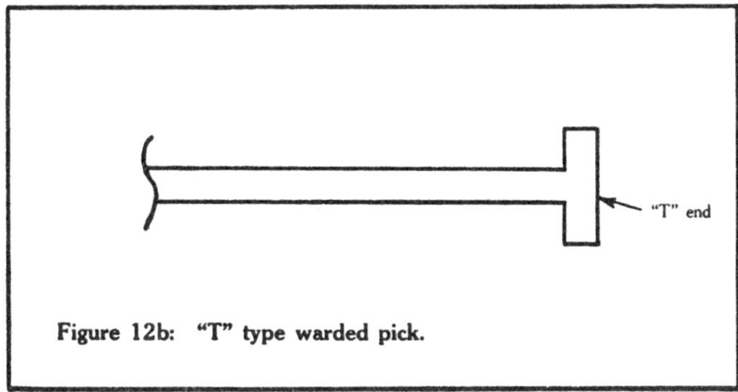

Figure 12b: "T" type warded pick.

To perform this BLT you must apply constant tension to the lock shackle while picking. This will cause the first set of retainers, when they are spread by the "T" of the pick, to bind against the sides of the shackle notch, and so not reseat when the "T" is removed, but rather be held. Once the first set of retainers is spread, the "T" is moved to the second set which are spread and the lock will open. Often, if the lock doesn't open then you can work back and forth between the two sets of retainers, since one set may have slipped. Other common faults are not applying enough binding tension on the shackle, or applying too much and causing the pick to bend or break. If the padlock is in service, tension may be easily applied by pulling down on it, but a rope or short chain should be carried in your kit for applying tension to unmounted lock shackles.

The concept of applying tension or movement force to parts

of the lock mechanism while manipulating other parts is essential to most types of BLT. The amount of tension in particular is very important, as was seen in bypassing the padlock retaining shackles. Although the point in time at which the shackle exits the retainer can often be heard as a little click, quite often it is manifested as a jump or change in the amount of tension feedback the lock is giving the operator, or the shackle may move ever so slightly.

If one set of retainers still applies spring tension after it is supposedly picked, you know that it is not really fully picked. This can be very frustrating. It does also matter which set of retainers is spread first. Try to detect and pick the more tightly bound of the two, since if the looser is picked first the shackle may move to the unlocked position only slightly, but it will bind the second set of retainers even more tightly then, with a risk of pick bending. Of course if you loosen tension slightly to avoid a tight bind, the looser set of retainers may then re-lock, so be sure to start on the tightest set. Increasing or decreasing the tension during the picking may also be helpful, because a "feel" will be built up between tension amounts and picks, and constantly varying the tension will make it easier to stumble onto this right combination. Of course to avoid all this hassle you can easily carry double-headed "T" picks, but the technique of tension and individual retainer manipulation is easy to learn and will help you to build up skills that are useful for other BLT's.

One final word concerns small suitcase and attache case locks that are warded type. These may present quite a problem not because of security of construction, but because the keyway is small and therefore very restrictive. Usually a "fits-all" tool doesn't work here, so you almost have to stock a key/tool for each make of lock. A good strategy in this case is to have five to six common keyblanks for the locks, and opening a specific lock then becomes a matter of selecting a blank that fills the keyway and impressioning it to fit the lock warding. Remember not to file away any portion of the blank that you suspect may be operating the boltwork -- cut it only to pass the wards. Since the average blank is of soft metal, it takes almost no time to make the necessary warding cuts. Although you wouldn't believe it would fit in such a small case, some of these locks also have a notched spring bolt retainer.

Usually the key will do the job of lifting both the retainer and throwing the bolt, but if not, a thin lifter pick inserted alongside the key may do the trick. If you are desperate, part of the side warding of the pick key can be filed away to accomodate a lifter pick, but this may seriously weaken the key.

This completes the coverage of warded locks and related BLT. Ideally all beginning lock specialists should start on warded locks, partially because of the ego boost you get by opening one, and also because a lock specialist that is stopped by a warded lock looks very foolish. 90% of the initial preparation here should go into properly sized tools, and only a little practice on skills.

CHAPTER 3
DISC TUMBLER LOCKS

Chronologically, the next lock to be developed was the lever tumbler lock, but this will be discussed later on. Instead let's take up the discussion of the more common disc tumbler lock. By the way, usually you think of combination locks when someone talks about tumblers, but a tumbler is actually any part of the lock that is directly manipulated by the key and has an unlocking function. Therefore, the tumbler for a disc lock is a part that resembles a disc, with an oblong slot cut in it's center.

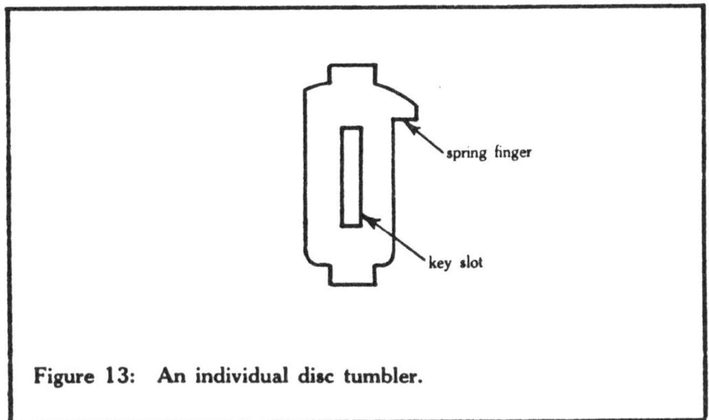

Figure 13: An individual disc tumbler.

Notice that the relative up and down position of the slot can be varied when the slot is being cut. Usually there are five increments of up and down position of slot relative to the edges of the disc, but notice that the dimensions of the slot do not vary, only its location within the disc. Now imagine that you take five of these discs (if you want you can even cut five nickle-sized discs out of card-board) and thread them onto a typical disc-tumbler key. If you don't have such a key (usually shorter than a house key but the same configuration) a house key will suffice. Make sure that you put each disc on so that the slot in it rests in the exact bottom or each "V" groove in the key.

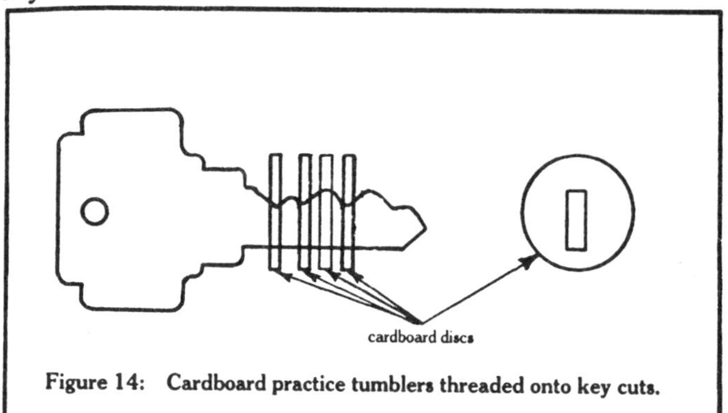

Figure 14: Cardboard practice tumblers threaded onto key cuts.

If you don't want to cut the cardboard, try drawing this concept by tracing the key on paper and adding the discs by sketching. As you can see now, the position of the slot in the disc, and the depth of cut in the "V" key bitting, are all related. In order for all of the discs to be at the same height, or in the same plane, high slots in discs must be placed in matching shallow key cuts, and low disc slots must have matching deep key cuts. Now look at figure 15 where the plug and cylinder are shown in side and top views.

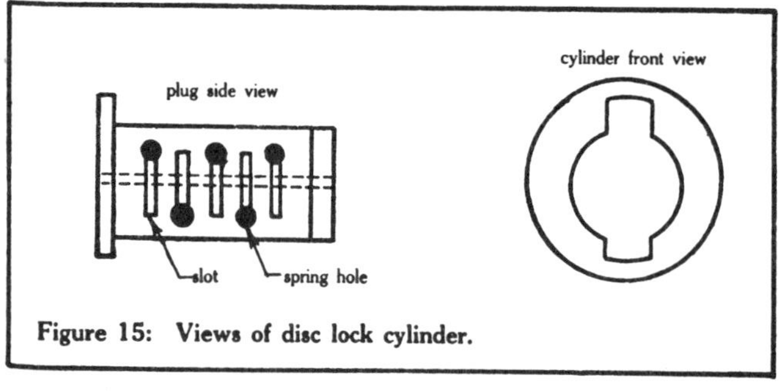

Figure 15: Views of disc lock cylinder.

Note the slots which extend completely through the plug. These hold the individual disc tumblers in alignment parallel to each other, and the tumblers slide up and down in these slots. Either end of any disc tumbler may project past the plug surface, depending on the combination of slot position and key cut depth. Note also the special fingers (see figure 13) cut in the discs with their matching holes in the plug that contain the disc springs. One end of the spring bottoms in the hole and the other end fits over the disc "finger" so that the spring exerts constant upward pressure on the disc.

Now turn attention to the cylinder or metal sleeve that the plug fits into. There are two grooves cut into the inner surface of the cylinder, located 180 degrees apart. When the plug is filled or loaded with disc tumblers and inserted into the cylinder, all of the tumbler ends project above the plug surface and into one of these grooves. Each individual tumbler end then prevents the plug from rotating inside the cylinder, even if only one projects. Now insert a key blank (no cuts) and observe how the tumblers ride up the wedge end of the key. When fully inserted, the key is threaded through all five disc slots, and the key is now pressing the discs down so that their opposite ends protrude from the bottom of the plug into the opposite cylinder groove. Since each disc has different height slots, all the disc ends protrude different amounts. One or two may even be flush if they are high slot discs that require a no-cut key bitting.

For instance, if the plug was loaded with all number three depth discs, and a key was cut with all number three height "V" cuts, then that key would retract all of the discs flush with both sides of the plug, no tumbler end would protrude to impede rotation, and the plug would turn, unlocking the lock. Obviously, however, such a choice of key codes would be poor since straight picks and wires could also align the disc tumblers properly. To provide maximum security a plug is usually loaded with an assortment of different depth discs. The problem for the lock specialist is then to align all the disc tumblers simultaneously so as to open the lock.

Before getting into bypass techniques however, some more background is needed. It is common to see disc locks with five tumblers, but six and seven are seen, and there are some ten tumbler locks. In other locks, some of the disc tumbler slots are cut wider than usual, and a double-bitted key is required to operate them.

There are also locks with two banks of disc tumblers located at 180 degrees to each other that look just the same when viewed through the keyway as the wide-slot disc type, but differ in that each tumbler in each bank moves independently. Therefore, when confronted with a lock that has what *appears* to be two sets of disc tumblers (they look like little staircase steps in the keyway) manipulating one side with a straight or feeler pick will usually tell the story since the wide-slot variety will move the opposite side when one side is moved, and the independent tumbler type will show one side not moving no matter how much the other side is manipulated. A look at the key will also tell the story since the wide-slot lock key will have quasi-symmetrical bitting on both sides such that the total of the two depths of any key cut positions is the same, and this is seen in figure 16. The independent tumbler lock key will show two different bitting profiles, one for each side of the key.

An interesting third type of double key profile is seen in some automotive pin tumbler locks in which the opposite side is a true mirror image of the first side, and this will be discussed in detail later. One other major point to remember is that all disc tumbler (and all pin tumbler as well) locks have a plug retainer

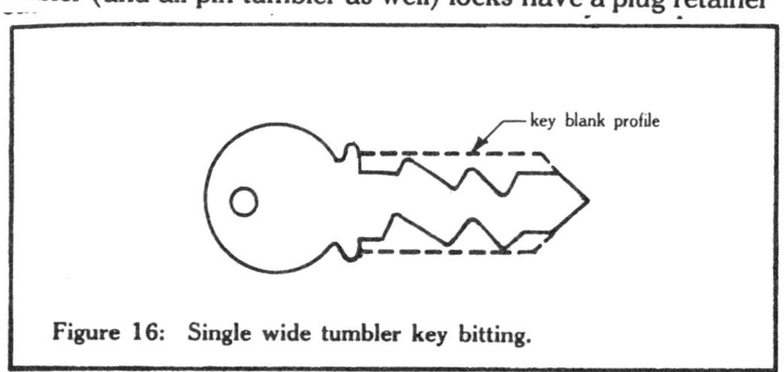

Figure 16: Single wide tumbler key bitting.

that prevents the plug from being withdrawn endwise -- the tumbler ends simply sliding in the cylinder grove. To prevent this unfortunate occurence, retainers are added, some in the form of cams screwed to the far end of the plug, snap rings that fit in grooves in the plug surface, or even plug and cylinder permanently brazed together at the factory. The most common type of retainer, however, is the disc retainer, an extra disc installed in a regular tumbler slot in the plug, but in the last

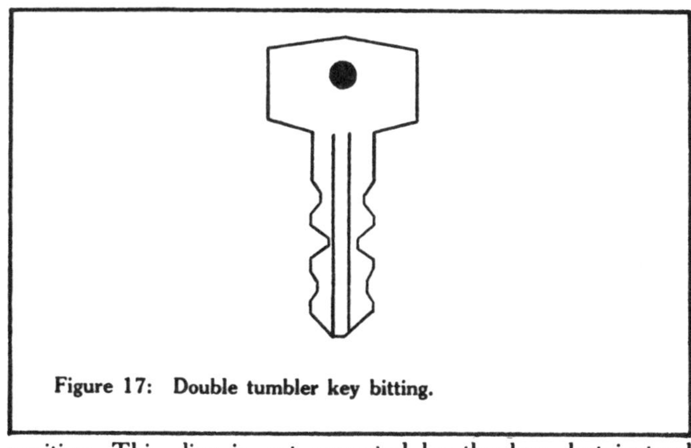
Figure 17: Double tumbler key bitting.

position. This disc is not operated by the key, but instead protrudes past the opposite side of the plug that the other tumblers do, sometimes at right angles to the usual tumbler travel. This tumbler also extends past the lock cylinder in its usual position and so prevents the plug from being pulled out of the lock. Some locks provide a hole in the front of the lock face that allows access to this retainer tumbler when the plug is partially or fully unlocked (of course not when locked) and the retainer may be retracted by using a wire that is tapered as shown in figure 18. This is inserted between the tumbler and the cylinder to wedge the retainer into the plug.

If you are following this carefully, you may see that nothing prevents a lock specialist from pushing, not pulling, the plug, into the cylinder, but just as the disc retainer prevents

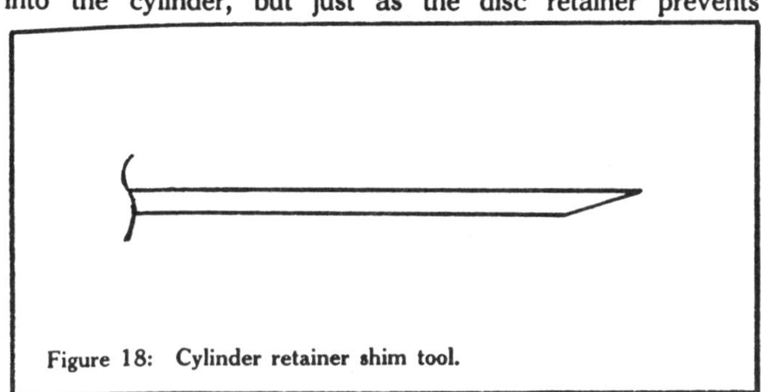
Figure 18: Cylinder retainer shim tool.

movement one way, the plug is usually cut with a shoulder as in figure 19 and the cylinder with a matching recess, which prevents pushing in the plug, and also prevents access to the tumbler ends from the front of the lock.

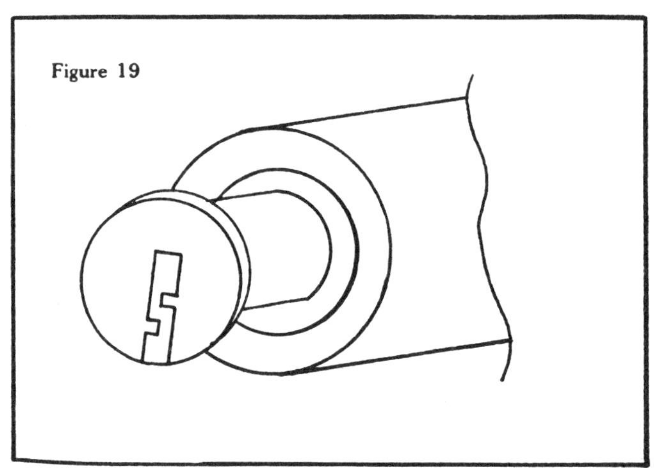
Figure 19

Note that if the tumbler ends were front-accessible, a thin shim of paper and/or metal could be inserted between the plug and cylinder as the tumblers were individually manipulated with a straight tool through the keyway, effectively unlocking the plug. This is important to see because later on a similar technique is discussed on pin tumbler locks. Just in back of the shoulder on the disc lock, most automotive or exterior application locks have a rubber O-ring riding in a groove on the plug, which seals the lock interior from the elements. One final point to consider is the method of cylinder mounting. Most cylinder exteriors are simply threaded and the lock inserted into a finish hole and locked at the back with matching washer and nut. Other retaining systems include "C" shaped clips for the cylinder (notably GM sidebar locks) and also external snap rings.

Common Applications

Disc tumbler locks are very common as accessory locks like showcase locks, telephone dials, office machines, cash registers, washroom towel dispensers, gas tank covers, switch locks, just about any recent low-security application. Conversely, they are almost never found as padlocks, exterior/interior passage sets, or other high usage applications. The automotive industry makes extensive use of a special disc tumbler called a sidebar which is covered later, and glovebox locks are usually disc locks.

Typical Key and Lockface Appearance

Most disc tumbler keys look just like pin tumbler keys with their side-cut warding and different depth "V" cuts, but they are an average of a quarter inch shorter, and may have smaller bows.

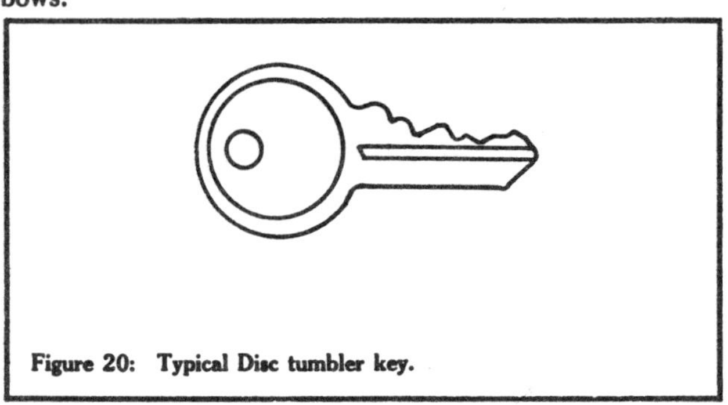

Figure 20: Typical Disc tumbler key.

As discussed earlier some disc locks have one set of discs and a key that is cut to contact both sides of the disc slot simultaneously, while other disc locks have two independent sets of discs and different sets of key bitting on each side of the key to operate the tumblers.

Now let's get into some action. I will assume that you have a copy of HOW TO MAKE YOUR OWN PROFESSIONAL LOCK TOOLS. You will also need a cheap disc lock and a piece of wood about 4″x4″x½″ to mount the lock in.

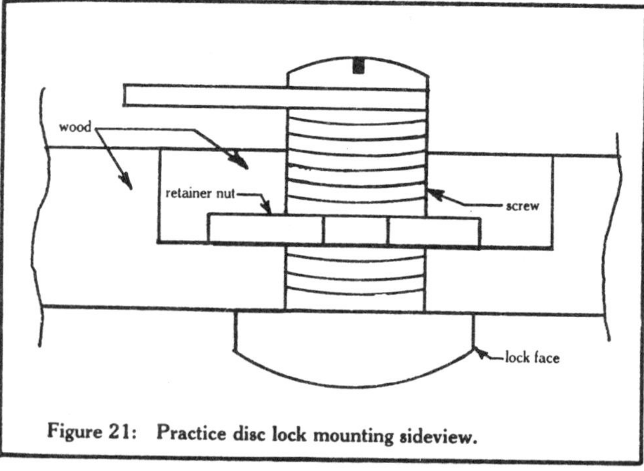

Figure 21: **Practice disc lock mounting sideview.**

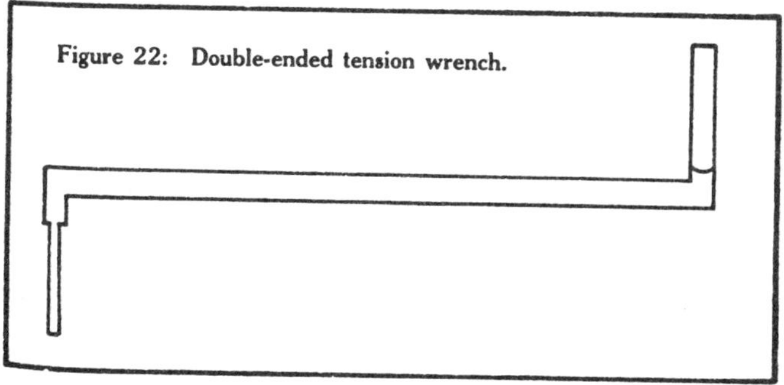

Figure 22: Double-ended tension wrench.

Once the lock is mounted, clamp the wood vertically in vise to provide the easiest working position. Select a tension wrench (a tool shaped like those in figure 22) into the lock keyway, making sure not to put the wrench in so that it will limit access by the raking tool which will be inserted next.

If you, like all of us, occasionally have trouble trying to find an un-obstructed piece of keyway to insert the tension wrench into, look for a shallow slot placed at the top or bottom of the keyway. This slot is where the stop on the key usually bottoms

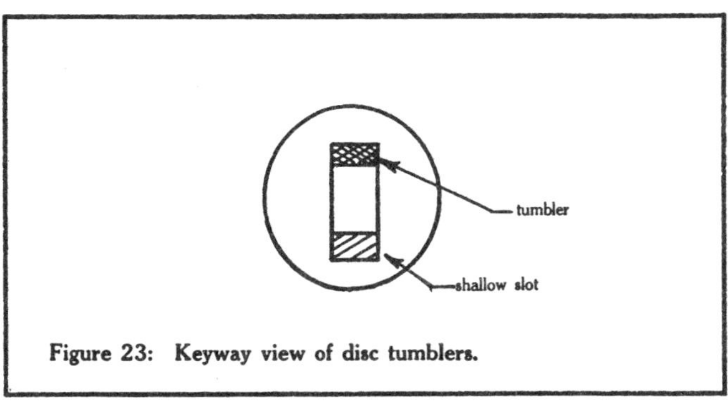

Figure 23: Keyway view of disc tumblers.

to provide precise alignment of the key and the tumblers, and a square ended tool will fit here easily without keyway obstruction, if you are careful not to apply excess tension.

Once the tension wrench is inserted, apply a little turning force or torque to the plug, in the direction the plug normally turns to unlock, until the tumblers bind. Now insert the rake pick (figure 24) under all of the tumblers (be careful because some locks have open keyway ends and the pick can be

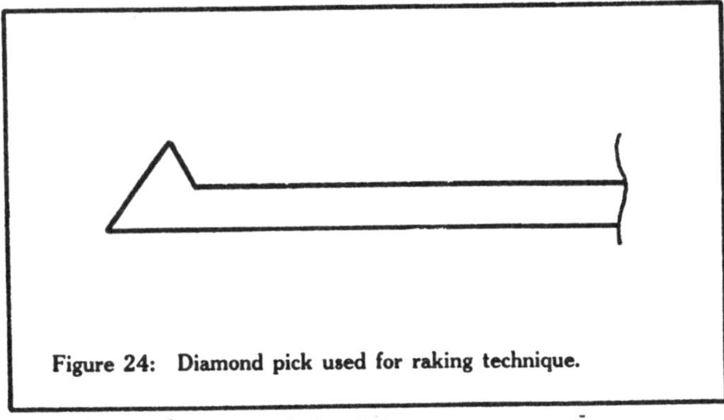
Figure 24: Diamond pick used for raking technique.

inserted into the space behind the lock).

See if the rake moves smoothly in and out of the lock, striking all the tumblers. If not, the rake may be too high and is binding on the wards. The proper grip is also important. While there are people who are successful with almost any type of tool hold, the best method seems to be holding the pick like a pencil and allowing it to pivot at the point where the fingers grab it. Tension is just as important -- too much tension will bind the tumblers excessively and the pick will just bend rather then move them, and too little tension or turning force will not make the tumblers bind at all. Above all, some tension must be constantly maintained throughout the entire bypass procedure.

So to recap, apply a light, constant turning tension with the tension wrench, hold the pick properly, inserting it under all the tumblers. Now work the rake in and out with a scrubbing action, being sure to contact each tumbler on both strokes, while allowing the pick to pivot in your finger-hold. If the pick is held too tightly, it will force the tumblers past their unlocked position. The theory of the raking method of bypass is that the scrubbing action of the pick moves the tumblers into the plug against their individual spring tensions until the other end of the tumbler encounters the other side of the cylinder. Normally, of course, the tumbler would proceed past the cylinder face and the end would protrude into the opposite cylinder grove, but since the specialist is applying a turning force to the plug, the plug and cylinder groove are misaligned and there is a little lip of cylinder edge that the tumbler end butts up against and can go no further.

nice amount of tension on the plug insures that the tumbler will essentially be trapped, with both ends butting up against both lips of the cylinder groove edge. Study figure 25 until this concept is clear. Obviously the amount of tension is vital to this method, as is a loose fitting between the lock parts. Once all of the tumblers have been trapped in this way, the lock plug will turn and unlock.

If you have trouble with this method, there are a few things to try. First, try varying the tension while raking, as long as it is not let off entirely. Often, reducing the tension while simultaneously taking a stroke will make the lock pop open. The usual first problem is applying too much tension so the tumblers are too friction-bound to move. Remember that the pick can only apply so much force before bending, so keep the tension light. Often a figure eight type of motion for the pick is also valuable, keeping the wrist loose and relying on finger pressure to move the pick. You can rest a finger on the lock mounting surface to steady your motion. Some specialists

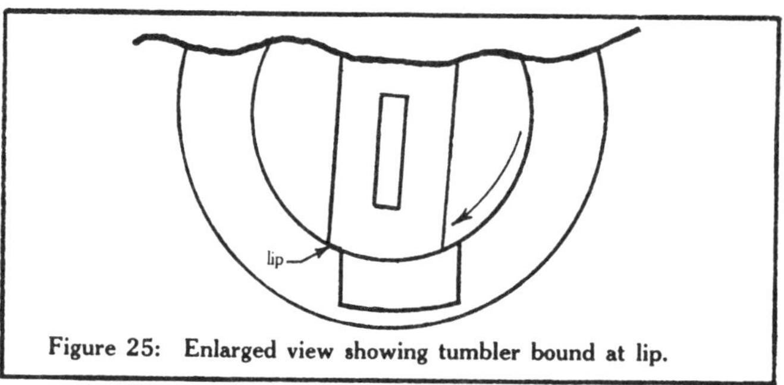

Figure 25: Enlarged view showing tumbler bound at lip.

advocate inserting the rake without tumbler contact, then abruptly and quickly pulling the rake out, contacting all the tumblers. This technique is called "ripping" a lock, and can be very effective. If you have now been successful, congratulations! Let's see you do it again. If not, check that you are trying to rotate the lock plug in the same direction that it normally goes to unlock, and also check the key bitting profile. A key cut with alternate high and low "V" cuts is more difficult to bypass with raking, try another lock with a "straighter" key.

When you finally succeed in bypassing a disc lock, take a walking tour of an office, school, or lock section of your

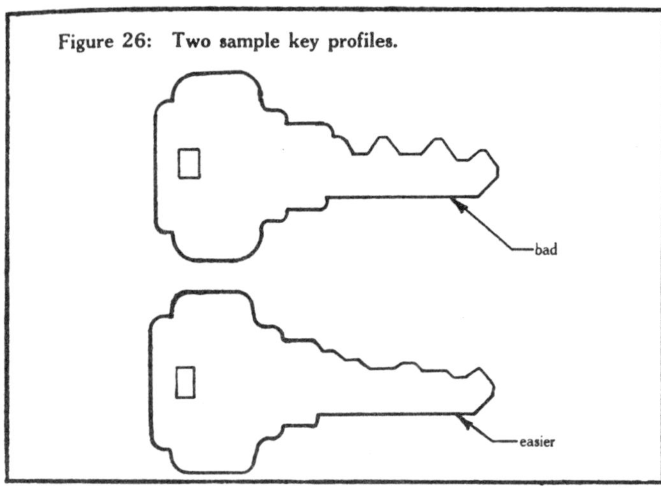

Figure 26: Two sample key profiles.

hardware store and notice how many locks are disc tumbler type. Just about all of these will yield to the same raking technique. As your technique develops you will build up a proper feel-ratio between amount of tension and proper pick manipulation. In time, you will be able to open a disc lock faster than a slow man with the right key. As mentioned earlier the reason for this lack of security is the very low tolerance that disc locks are made to. Most of the parts are either stamped or cast, and consequently the finished lock has a lot of play in it. Play or loose fit is deadly to any lock security, because a specialist can exploit it.

CHAPTER 4
HOW TO MOUNT PRACTICE LOCKS

Now that you are a beginning lock specialist, let's have a little discussion on mounting practice locks. The best skill practice is done when a lock is in it's usual "in sevice" position and making a mounting board will facilitate this practice. You should mount a disc tumbler, a rim or mortise pin tumbler, a lever tumbler, a warded lock, and a warded padlock. You can buy all of these new, or look through second-hand stores and salvage yards, especially on the warded mortise locks which are hard to find. Be sure to purchase the cheapest lock available since the cheaper locks are low tolerance and easier to bypass.

BILL OF MATERIALS

Plywood

(1) 12″ x 18″ x ½″ (back)
(1) 10¼″ x 18″ x ½″ (front)
(1) 1¾″ x 18″ x ½″ (spacer)

Lumber

(2) 2″ x 4″ x 18″ (sides)
(1) 2″ x 4″ x 8″ (lock spacer)
(1) 2″ x 4″ x 9″ (shelf)

Hardware

(1) staple and hasp with mounting hardware
(2) butt hinges 1″ x 3″
(50) 1″ finishing nails
glue # 602
(8) cup hooks

Locks As Per Text

(1) Disc Tumbler Cam
(1) Rim or Mortise Pin Tumbler
(1) Lever Tumbler
(1) Warded Mortise
(1) Warded Padlock

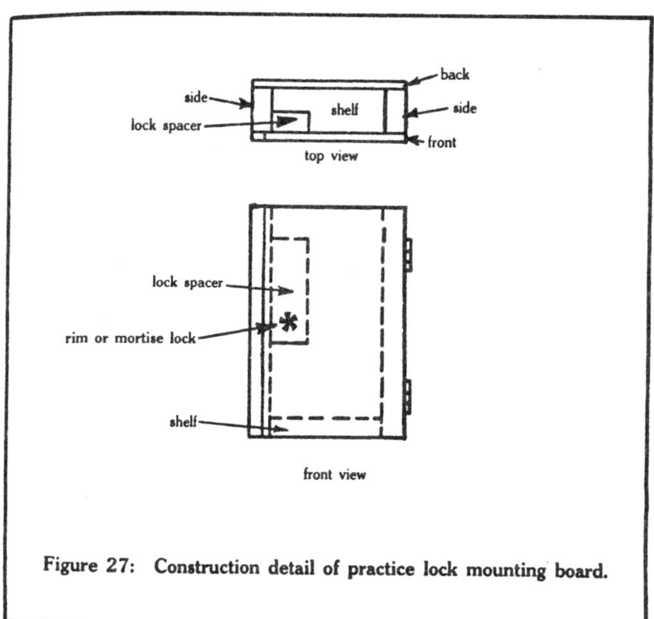

Figure 27: Construction detail of practice lock mounting board.

Assemble as shown in figure 27 using finishing nails and glue.

Make sure to provide at least one sixteenth inch clearance between the door and the jamb. The 8″ long 2 x 4 provides sufficient thickness to mount the rim and mortise locks, and should be installed in the middle of the door edge. The 9″ 2 x 4 is nailed into the box as a shelf, but don't mount it in the way of the spacer blocks, or future protruding lock hardware. Follow all manufacturers directions for mounting the locks. Any order or spacing is good -- figure 27 just shows one such arrangement. When completed, the unit should be mounted on a wall, workbench, bookshelf, door, or other vertical surface, with the rim cylinder at the height it would normally be on a door. This allows for realism in practice. It is funny how soon technique evaporates when working in real-life conditions. The appropriate key for each lock may be mounted on a nail or cuphook placed on the side of the box next to the lock.ck.

Try to mount the box in a traffic pattern so that you will pass by it frequently and hopefully stop to practice. You should try for two fifteen minute sections of practice a day. After your technique is developed you might try subduing the light while working, or even use a flashlight if you are really gung-ho. This will quickly show you that a flashlight must be held by some third hand arrangement. A very good method for practice is to start a stopwatch, hang it inside the case and lock the door. The time pressure is good for technique, and the watch will tell you how long the opening required. Another thing to try is opening two locks on the same door, since many doors have a key-in-knob and an auxiliary deadbolt for added security. It is also a good idea to concentrate initially on the pin tumbler locks since these are the most common, and the technique built up is transferable to other lock types. Perhaps a good incentive to open the door on the practice cabinet is to put a picture of your girl or boyfriend inside the cabinet.

One of the first things you find out when using a lock tool is that one hand is always "frozen" to the tension wrench during the picking process. For things like holding flashlights, if you can't grow a third arm and hand (and who can) try a magnetic mount flashlight. Another nifty dodge is taping a penlight directly to your arm, or holding it in your mouth like a cigar. Lots of other possibilities suggest themselves if you use a little thought. Furthermore, if you get tired during the picking process, it is good to have a large map type push pin and a couple of knotted rubber bands. By pushing the pin into the wood door and applying tension to the wrench via the rubber bands, you can leave the job. A small magnet will substitute for the push pin on metal-clad doors. (See figure 28.)

Still another topic under the frozen-hand problem is tool access. With certain styles of BLT you may have to make tool changes while maintaining tension. Informally, I carry a small leather case of tools and I access these by draping the open case over my knee. Other solutions are possible though, like a tool case with double faced adhesive tape on the back to adhere it to doors or walls. A pouch for tools mounted on a forearm strap would be excellent, and also offer concealment. Velcro is also good; put the fuzzy component anywhere you want to conceal and/or access the tool case, and put the hook component on the case itself. A word of caution, due to the need for tool changes, many of the commercially available pen pick sets, or jackknife-type pick sets can be a real hassle, requiring two hands to switch the bit on such tools. Try to avoid these because they also offer a lot of pick profiles that are rarely used, and this adds a lot of weight to a tool handle that must be easily manipulated.

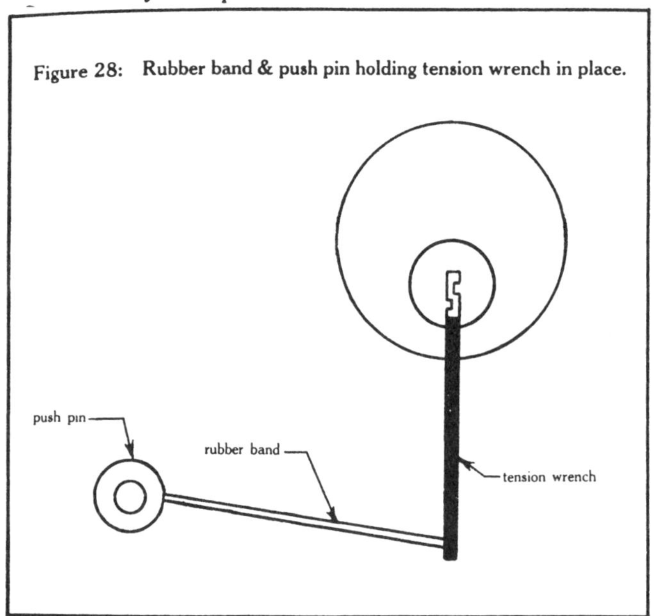

Figure 28: Rubber band & push pin holding tension wrench in place.

Since the discussion is stalled on subjects *relating* to BLT, let's talk about a procedure that should be followed with any BLT attempt. I'll assume that you have already checked to make sure the lock is not already unlocked, that the door is not just swelled and stuck in the jamb, that the lock in question is still being used, and is in good condition (I spent an unsuccessful fifteen minutes once attempting to bypass a lock that was so worn even the right key required manipulation to operate the lock), and that other means of entry are not available, like windows and such.

First off, examine the keyway to determine the type of lock. A stamped metal plate with a keyway cut out usually means a warded lock, or a lever tumbler lock, whereas keyways with circular shapes and formed wards showing are usually pin tumbler, disc tumbler, or wafer tumbler locks (Schlage). Wafer tumbler locks are covered later. On padlocks especially, the keyways cut into free rotating cores are usually warded locks. They are lever tumbler locks if the free rotating core has a

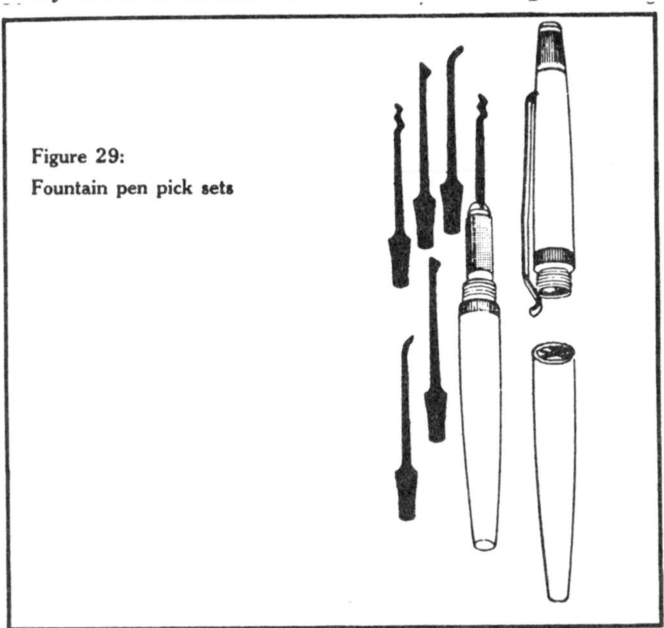

Figure 29:
Fountain pen pick sets

matching slot cut in the side of it's retainer. If the core is immobile, it is a pin tumbler lock.

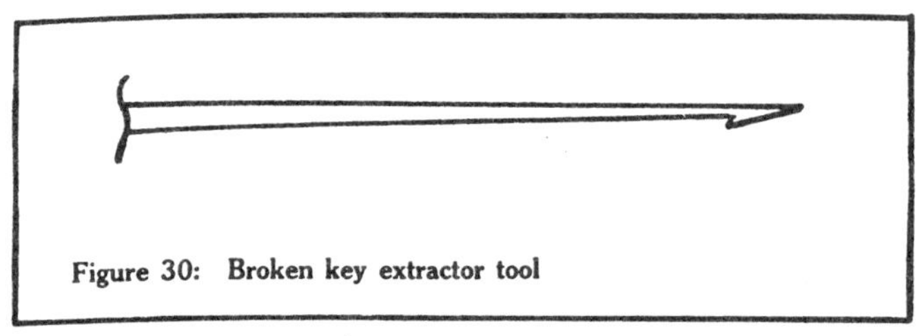
Figure 30: Broken key extractor tool

matching slot cut in the side of it's retainer. If the core is immobile, it is a pin tumbler lock.

Next, examine the keyway for foreign objects like broken-off keys or toothpicks. A favorite trick of burglars to deny owner access and avoid suprises is to fill the keyway with broken off toothpicks.

Examine also the pin ends or disc slots if possible. If they are not all visible it may mean that a tumbler is jammed up inside the cylinder or plug which would make picking impossible. It may also be that the plug was loaded with less than a full set of tumblers, a practice employed by poor locksmiths, which of course compromises security. It may also be a different type of lock than you think. The individual sections in this book on lock fronts will provide additional recognition information.

Next, check the brand name, if visible -- this may indicate if special lock features are present, like mushroom pins in CORBIN and RUSSWIN locks and hardened drill inserts in SEGAL and SCHLAGE locks. These brands are by no means inclusive.

Next, insert a tension wrench or other tool into the keyway and attempt to rotate the plug. The more play or rotation in the plug the lower the precision of manufacture and the easier the lock is to bypass. While attempting to turn the plug, also try to ascertain which way the plug turns to unlock, which is very important. Wrong-way plug rotation during picking will never bypass the lock. Most plugs have a positive stop machined into the boltwork cam or cylinder, and the feel of this abrupt stop while rotating the plug is quite different from the creeping stop that you feel when the tumblers individually impede plug rotation. There are some rules that can be followed for plug rotation determination, but there are always exceptions. Most mortise and key-in-knob pin tumbler locks rotate so that the cut edge of the key (if installed in the proper key cut edge-up position) rotates towards the door edge, CORBIN and RUSSWIN locks are the exception, however. Padlocks and office machine pin and disc tumbler locks usually turn clockwise or in both directions to unlock. Other types of accessory locks will turn in one direction only to lock, and the other to unlock.

Another valuable piece of information for the initial survey is the amount of lubricant in the lock. Your sense of smell will give the answer, or large amounts of dust adhering to the lock face will indicate a recent copious oiling. If you encounter a lock that is dirty, dusty or gritty, cleaning it will ease the bypass operation. Also, any lock that has been over-oiled should be cleaned. Use a squirt can of naptha or lighter fluid or use a hypodermic or ear syringe with naptha to flush out the keyway. Do at least two flushings and work the tumblers up and down between the flush with a straight tool. Do not use gasoline, WD-40, or LPS-1 for cleaning because they all leave a residue after evaporation. Remember also that the cleaning process also leaves physical evidence (i.e., a noticeable odor) of tampering, not a good practice for the black bag operator. After flushing twice, blow dry with an ear syringe, lips and lungs, a short piece of rubber tubing, or use a pipe cleaner. The object is to dry the lock and also float away any grit remaining. Some photographic and industrial supply houses have inert gas compressed in a can for blowing away dust and chips, which also works well. The majority of locks will, however, be reasonably clean and dry. In fact, if the lock shows excessive and recent lubrication, start to worry because a malfunctioning lock is usually doused with lubricant by it's owner in an attempt to make it work, and nothing is harder to manipulate than a lock that won't function well even if the right key is used.

Now that the lock is dry and clean, should you add a little lubricant to aid the picking process? Some specialists like to work a lock dry -- the feel is better, according to them. Others, however, prefer a litle lubricant, especially for the individual tumbler lifting techniques, and if you want to try this, use a short squirt of powdered graphite.

While it occurs to me, I should mention that in surveying a lock on an exterior residential application, try looking for spare keys in flower pots, planters, under door mats, in breezeways or enclosed porches, on tops of ledges, in mailboxes under hollow stair units, etc. A general rule is to think of where you might hide a key, then look there. Loompanics Unlimited also offers several good books on hiding places, and picking up a few of these may well save you some trouble as well as improving your search technique for black bag jobs.

Finally, in the initial survey, try to analyze the type of locking bolt or latch mechanism used, and particularly whether a deadbolt auxiliary slide (which is a small, parallel bar that prevents the latch from responding to external pressure) exists, or if the latch is key deadlocked (cannot be retracted into the lock case by endwise pressure). If no deadlocking feature exists, the easiest bypass may well be an attack on the bolt.

So much for the initial lock survey. Try to get in the habit of doing this whole routine, especially for locks that usually give you trouble. If it becomes automatic, then you won't overlook an obvious move that may have saved you some time.

CHAPTER 5
LEVER TUMBLER LOCKS

The next lock type to consider is the little-seen lever tumbler lock. This design was actually the next step in lock evolution after warded construction, and offered far greater security potential. In fact, the lever tumbler was developed to replace the warded lock. In England, circa 1817, perfect burglaries were rampant, all committed with the aid of lock-picking tools of the day. As a result of an especially daring robbery, the British Government offered a prize of 100 pounds to the inventor of a pick-proof lock. The result was the patenting of the Chubb lever lock in 1818.

A similar lock design (actually the first lever lock) was also patented by Joseph Brahmah who started a grand tradition in lock advertising that still continues today, the awarding of money prizes to the first individual to successfully bypass a new lock design. This first prize of 200 ginueas was awarded to Mr. Hobbs, an American lock specialist who opened the Brahmah lock in 25 min. using a tension wrench, lifter, and four other tools. Quite frankly, I think the other four tools, pictured in the *Times* article discussing the feat, are merely included to throw the average reader off the track -- the wrench and lifter would have sufficed. Despite Mr. Hobb's success, the lever lock soon became the standard of security, and was constantly improved, but never to the point of making it unpickable by specialists.

Applications

Today the lever lock still survives in its role as a high security lock, since bank vault safety deposit boxes use this type of lock almost exclusively. In this role it is so secure that the average locksmith cannot spend the necessary time to bypass it, and few are really skilled in this technique, so he merely screws a special sheet metal screw right into the keyway and wrenches the door off the box, using a special tool called a nose puller. Lever locks are also found in low security applications like early office equipment, chests and cabinets, some luggage locks, and so on. Some early mortise door locks are also lever locks.

Keyway

Lever locks have distinctive keyways, simply a slot cut into the face of a metal cylinder end which is in turn encased in a rolled metal collar with a matching small slot cut in its side.

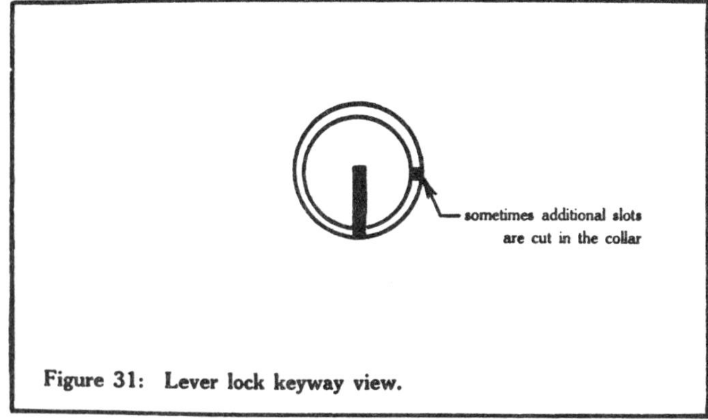

Figure 31: Lever lock keyway view.

This cylinder or thimble or barrel or nose rises above the level of the mounting surface usually, and is distinctive in that the nose is free to rotate whether a key is inserted or not. The nose actually serves as a carrier for the key, and also limits access. The key, though encased in the nose, usually operates the boltwork directly, just as in warded locks.

Keys

Lever tumbler keys are called flat keys in the trade, and they are just that -- flat stamped profiles without side warding cuts. They have one cut called the throat cut near the bow that allows the key blade to pass the rolled edge that retains the nose, and a series of rectangular cuts of varying depth near the tip. These cuts raise the tumblers to their various heights.

Operation

As in disc tumbler locks, where the disc is the varying height mechanism, in lever tumbler locks, the lever (see figure 32) is moved to varying heights, against the pressure of a spring, by the key bitting, and the bolt stump is then free to be pushed through the aligned slots in the interior of the levers, from one large cutout area to another.

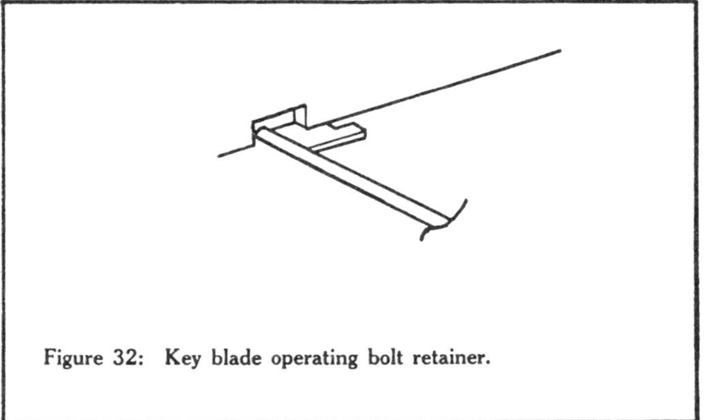

Figure 32: Key blade operating bolt retainer.

The bolt movement is accomplished by key also, the end of the key engaging the bolt just as in warded construction. Notice that the key contacts and elevates the tumblers by rotation, not by being shoved into the lock as in a disc tumbler. Therefore, the key bitting consists of rectangular cuts, and no wedge profiles are necessary. Note also that the nose is a rotating carrier that holds the key in the proper height relationship to the tumblers, and revolves it around a precise axis. As the key is rotated, the bitting comes in contact with the bottom of each tumbler, which is cut in a radius. Also notice that the tumblers may come in stacks of two, three, and even up to fifteen, each with a common pivot point, and an individual spring. When the key reaches its TDC (top dead center) or highest point of rotation, it lifts the levers varying amounts depending on the depth of the key bitting at each tumbler position. This height corresponds with the height positioning of the gate or notch cut into each tumbler that connects the two large cutout areas in the tumbler. Therefore, the height of gate varies and is matched to key bitting depth to get all of the tumblers gates lining up at the same height to allow passage of the stump (a finger or post projecting from the bolt at right angles).

There is one other system, in which the gates are all cut at the same height on the tumblers, and the tumbler bottoms that contact the key are cut away to get height variations that must be matched up with proper key bitting. Notice that the tumblers must all line their gates up before the stump can pass through, and if even one is low or high, the stumps' passage will be obstructed. Also notice that after the key has been turned past TDC the levers will lower, under spring action, to their resting heights, and the bolt will be caught in either the locked side of tumbler cutout, or the unlocked side, so all lever locks of simple design are dead locking in function.

BLT for the lever lock introduces a new class of technique, individually lifting the tumblers to their proper height. The tension wrench used for lever locks varies depending on the type of lock. In some locks, just the key end is used to move the bolt once it is unlocked, but there are models where the nose has a cam attached to its back end that directly acts on the bolt. In cases like these, a wrench that will move the nose, yet allow effective pick access, is sufficient. In the locks where the key itself moves the bolt (and these are the most common) a special tension wrench is required, as shown in figure 33.

These "Z" shaped wrenches must be sized to the length of the nose. If dimension "A" corresponds to the length of the key from cylinder cut to tip, then that is the right size wrench. To allow room for pick manipulation outside the lock, the "A" dimension should be no greater than that. Commercial picks usually come in four or five "A" dimensions, and I strongly suggest you buy a set rather than trying to make one. If you must have a handmade tool, try bending the profile from .040 music wire and then grinding each side flat for lock clearance. Grinding the wrench profile from a piece of flat stock is also possible, but time consuming. If you want to do this, either buy

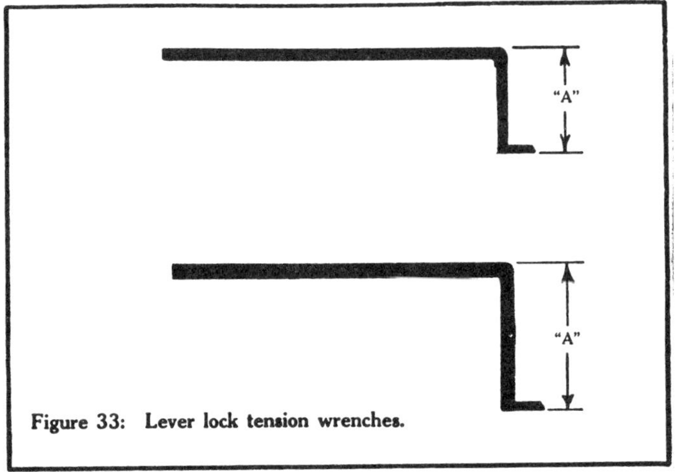

Figure 33: Lever lock tension wrenches.

flat stock at an industrial supply store, or find a hardware store that carries cabinet scrapers (a piece of tempered steel about the size of a playing card) and grind the wrench profile from it. For lifter tools, your usual set that works disc and pin tumblers will also work levers.

The theory of lever tumbler picking involves exerting unlocking tension on the bolt, which in turn will cause the stump to bear against the inner edge of the locked position tumbler cutout. Once tension is applied, the specialist inserts and uses the lifter to raise an individual tumbler until its gate is lined up with the stump. Since stumps are usually light parts that can be bent off perpendicular with extreme bolt pressure the tumbler to start lifting initially is the one at the back of the lock, since if the stump is bent, it will contact this tumbler the heaviest, and the others hardly or not at all. When the stump and gate align then, the stump will enter into the gate slightly, and catch on the stump. If tension is not released, this slight entrance (only a few thousandths of an inch) will serve to hold the tumbler in the unlocked position, even if the lifting pressure is removed. The feel of the tumbler gate aligning with the stump may be quite noticable, and may even be slightly audible. Often the tension wrench will signal this event by jumping slightly. The entrance or aligning may also be felt as a slight lessening in lifting resistance, which will immediately increase if the tumbler is over lifted.

Warning: *do not over lift any tumbler*, because this means you must start over. That is probably what took Hobbs so long. In fact, some lever tumblers are provided with a special tuumbler that detects over-lifting and immediately locks the bolt from further movement, so be careful.

Now once the first tumbler has been lifted to unlocked position, proceed to the next tumbler, working from the back to the front. The tension may be slightly decreased at this point, but not too much. The feel of subsequent tumblers entering their gates will be progressively less than the first tumbler, again owing to the bending angle of the stump. Eventually all of the tumblers are lined up, and the bolt moves, unlocking.

A few comments are in order here. First, a lever tumbler may have one tumbler cut as deep as possible, adjacent to one cut as shallow as possible, owing to its unique design. This is not possible with disc or pin tumblers, as will be explained later. Obviously that is good security, because for the pick to raise one tumbler sufficiently high without touching and possibly misaligning an adjacent tumbler, the lifter must have a high hook to put as much space between working tip and shank. A high-low-high-low-high combination would be very difficult indeed, just as it is with pin tumbler locks, as much as they are able to do this. Second, let me emphasize again that over-lifting is fatal. The only way to get a tumbler back down is to release tension until it falls, and other picked tumblers may also fall in the process, which can be very discouraging. Conversely, if a lever happens to drop back down while you are working it (as the pick leaves it), go immediately to the back of the lock and test each tumbler for alignment. The tumblers must be picked in order since they bind most strongly in the usual back to front order.

Occasionally, however, you may encounter a lock where, say, the third tumbler will not budge when you attempt to lift it. First, try backing off the tension a hair. If still no go, you can be sure you have a lock with an uneven tumbler line -- not all of the tumblers edges equally in line with the stump. If this happens, you can take advantage of this lack of manufacturing tolerance. Notice that if you apply a medium tension to the bolt and feel to see which of the tumblers is the most bound or the hardest to lift, that tumbler will be the first, and the easiest to bypass since none of the other tumblers are preventing the stump from moving as much as the most bound tumbler. In other words, play exists between the looser tumblers and the stump, so therefore the stump is free to advance slightly, once the tumbler that is blocking it is picked, namely, the most bound tumbler and so on. Examine figure 34 and notice that the tumbler that has the smallest arc or radius cut into its bottom also has a high gate and requires little lifting, while those with larger arcs have lower gates and require a lot of lifting.

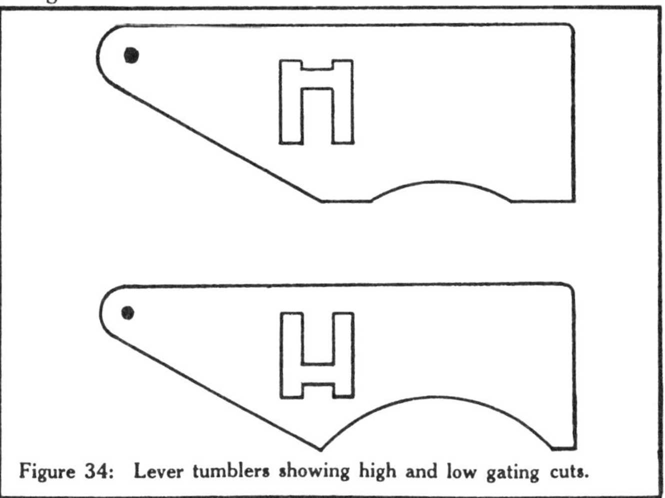

Figure 34: Lever tumblers showing high and low gating cuts.

This is the second system of gating height, where the tumbler is cut away at the bottom to provide gate height differences. By probing the lock and feeling for the relative amount of curvature on each lever, it is possible to get a mental picture of how far each lever must be lifted to align the gate and stump. You may need a special lifter pick with a very slim tip to feel between adjacent tumblers, but this can be a worthwhile technique.

Before we leave lever locks, let me warn you about one and two-lever chest and luggage locks. These present real problems in opening because of the small keyway and therefore limited access. If you really expect to shiv a lot of baggage surreptitiously, carry around a good assortment of luggage keys and a file for on the spot alteration. Hopefully one will fill the keyway and can be impressioned (coating of soot) to operate the lock as a *tension wrench only*. The levers must then be lifted just like usual.

Probing the lock for a part that seems to be spring loaded will offer clues as to the type of lever and number. Often a length of .015—.025 music wire bent to an approximate "Z" configuration will serve as a good tension wrench, and another length suitably bent will serve as a lifter. A handy thing to try is filing away the warded *sides* of a key to allow lifter pick access. Always also suspect that what appears to be a small lever lock may in fact be merely a warded lock with a spring retainer that must be lifted before the bolt can be moved. Notice that the amount of lifting for a retainer is not critical, where for a lever lock it would be.

CHAPTER 6
PIN TUMBLER LOCKS

On to the pin tumbler, the lock you will most frequently bypass, and therefore the one to study the most. The pin tumbler design is the most secure of the lock types in widespread use. It is found on exterior and interior doors, automobiles, office equipment, furniture, chests and cabinets, padlocks, accessory locks, etc. The list is endless. The pin tumbler was first patented and marketed in the period 1860-1868, and the design is essentially unchanged today. Let's get right to the mechanism.

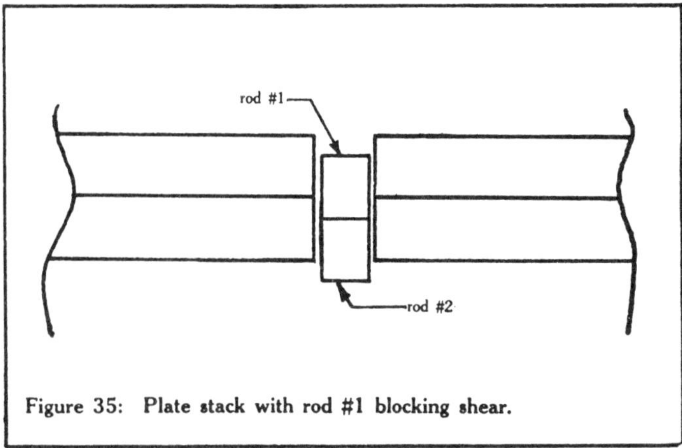

Figure 35: Plate stack with rod #1 blocking shear.

In figure 35 a stack of two brass plates has a hole drilled through it. Now let's drop two short pieces of brass rod into the

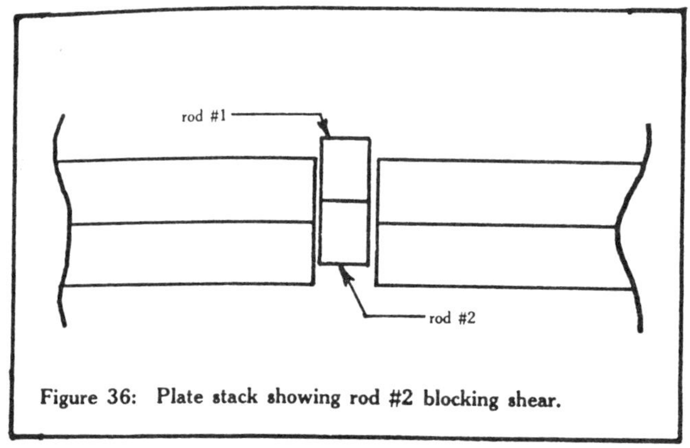

Figure 36: Plate stack showing rod #2 blocking shear.

hold. If we try to move or slide the plates in opposite directions, rod #1 would bind in the hole and prevent all but a few thousands of an inch motion. Notice also in figure 36 if the rod stack is moved up, #2 rod would then bind.

If, however, the rod stack is lifted just enough so the break between the rods is at the level where the plates meet (which we will call the shear line), the plates will now slide in opposite directions, each plate carrying one of the rods in its hole. Now let's add a little ledge to support the bottom pin as in figure 37 and also a spring to push down on the top pin.

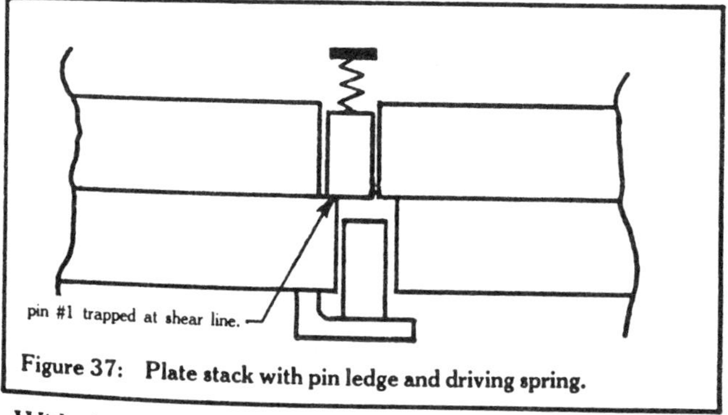

Figure 37: Plate stack with pin ledge and driving spring.

With these additions it is now necessary to lift and hold the pin stack at shear while *simultaneously* sliding the plates -- if not the spring would push both pins back down to rest on the ledge. Now, watch carefully as we bend both plates in a circle.

The end result is our friend the cylinder with a plug inside, both of which have a communicating set of holes, and a pin each. The ledge is in the plug, and the top spring is in the cylinder. Now examine your door lock and key. Identify the plug and cylinder of your lock, and insert the key halfway into the plug. Note that the little ledge which keeps the pins from being pushed out the bottom of the plug holes by the spring, is really a ward in the keyway, with an attendent cut in the key to pass the ward. So the ward does double duty by retaining the bottom of the pin stack, and limiting keyway access. Now insert the key the rest of the way into the lock and notice that the bottom end of the bottom pin will come to rest in the bottom of each "V" cut on the key.

By the way, did you notice that there are five holes drilled in the plug/cylinder, each in line with the other going from front to back, and also that each set of holes has its own set of top and bottom pins? If you didn't catch this, stop for a moment and examine the illustrations. To continue, notice on your key that the "V" cuts all have different depths. This depth is calculated to correspond to the length of the bottom pin so that with the key inserted, the top of the bottom pin will be exactly at the shear line between plug and cylinder.

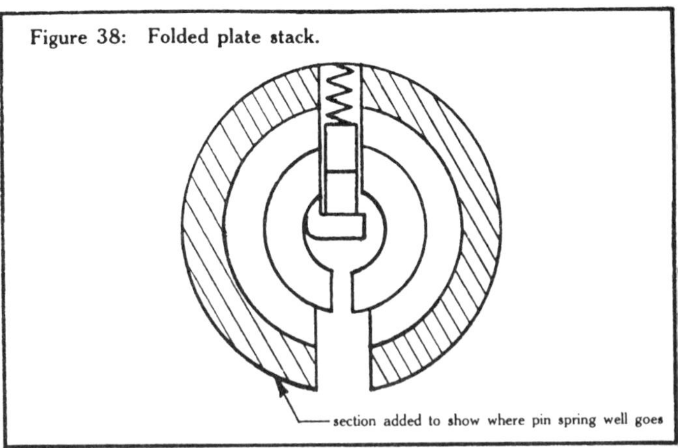

Figure 38: Folded plate stack.

Remember the discussion of plug retainers in the section on disc tumbler locks? The same type of retainer is necessary on pin tumbler locks because with the key inserted, and all of the bottom pins lifted exactly to the shear line (the top of the plug) the plug is then in effect a solid piece or rod of metal, and can easily be turned in the cylinder, and even withdrawn. If it were withdrawn, the tops of the bottom pins would show flush with the plug. Some unskilled locksmiths even re-key a lock by cutting the key combination, inserting it and adding bottom pins of any length into the holes in the plug, then filing the ends of the pins off flush with the top of the plug. (This is not important though, let's continue with a discussion of key combinations.)

The average lock manufacturer sets up his tooling so that there are definite steps or graduations of cut depth and matching heights of bottom pin. These can be as little as four or five steps, and as much as ten. Therefore, a high quality lock with seven sets of pins (tumblers) and seven depths of cut may have a possible theoretical number of 7^7, or 823, 543 combinations. Furthermore, if a pin is misaligned by as little as .005 of an inch (most step increments tend to be as much as .015—.020) the lock will catch and remain locked. Obviously, keeping a tryout set of keys cut to all of the possible combinations would develop strong arms quickly, so how does the average FBI specialist commit the average black bag job?

Figure 37 is back to the two plate stack with the top pin lifted above the shear line slightly, and force applied to slide the two plates apart. Notice that this sliding force would take the form of attempted plug rotation with a tension wrench, in a regular lock, the familiar tension concept. Now as the tension is applied, the plates (plug and cylinder) will misalign, if only for a few thousands of an inch before the other pin stacks that are not being lifted bind and stop further movement. This slight misalignment produces a tiny lip or ledge to form where the two holes do not line up. In figure 39 the top pin is being pressed down by the spring, but since it is catching on this lip and not going below the shear line, it is effectively picked.

Notice also that the bottom pin is free and has dropped back down onto the keyway ward. One can now proceed to the other pin stacks and manipulate or individually lift them also, until they are all held by the lip or ledge created by tension on the plug (the sliding force exerted on the plates).

Now, you may say, does this lip exist on all locks? The answer is yes. The manufacturer must always supply some space between the plug and cylinder, and also between the pin and the pin hole to prevent accumulated grit, temperature

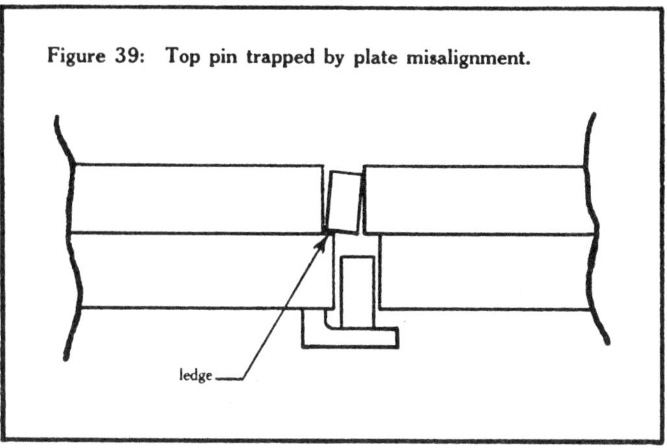
Figure 39: Top pin trapped by plate misalignment.

change, or physical deformation of parts to freeze up the lock. It is this tolerance that the lock specialist takes advantage of. The sloppier the fit, the bigger the ledge created by tension or turning force. Mass production costs also rise drastically when high tolerances are to be produced, so the cheapest locks are generally the easiest to bypass.

In the initial lock survey section, I taught you to attempt rotation of the plug -- the more rotation the easier the lock is to bypass. This is again the amount of lip that will be created by misaligning the plug and cylinder holes, so the more rotation, the easier the lock to bypass. After you have selected the proper tension wrench, inserted it into the keyway, and applied

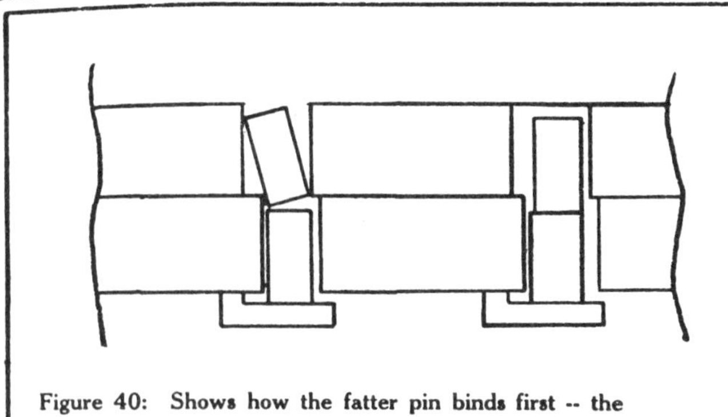
Figure 40: Shows how the fatter pin binds first -- the thinner pin does *not* bind.

tension in the unlocking direction, which pin should be individually lifted first? As another consequence of tolerances in mass production, the diameters of the top and bottom pins will all be slightly different. Thus there will be a fattest and a thinnest pin. As turning tension is applied, the fattest pin will bind first, and should therefore be lifted first.

When it is lifted to shear, the plug will turn a little more and bind the next fattest pin, and so on. If you lift a pin that is not the fattest one initially, the plug may still turn slightly, but that turning will then bind the fattest pin so tightly that lifting would be impossible, and the pick would only bend. So take the pins in the order of fat to thin. The best way to make sure you have the fattest pin is to apply a moderate turning tension and lift each pin in turn looking for the most resistence. If two pins seem to be evenly bound during this survey, release tension gradually while checking them both, and one will eventually loosen up -- this is the thinner of the two. *AS ALWAYS*, the amount of tension applied is vital to the success of the bypass. The common fault of too much tension will cause you to bend picks, and too little will get you nowhere fast. The specialist frequently varies tension during the picking process, both to aid in the bypass and to gain information about pin diameter and position of pin stacks relative to the shear line.

Sometimes a sudden variation in tension will pop a lock open, especially during the raking BLT which incidentally works quite well with pin tumblers as well as disc locks. There are two schools of thought on tension wrench configurations. The so-called "American" system favors a tool with a springy shank and a working end that is a (more or less) loose fit in the keyway. The "European" system is just the opposite -- tight fitting working end, and a solid unbending shank. There are good and bad points for each. The American wrench is easier to insert and fit to various keyways, and leaves no discernable scratches on the plug wall. The relatively constant tension level afforded by a springy shank is also good for beginners, ideal for raking BLT, and only three of four widths of working end need be carried because of the wedge fit. Its disadvantages are loss of pin feel via the plug, and difficulty in maintaining light turning tensions. The tight fit of the European wrench means having many more widths of working end available -- thus, a larger tool kit and a fitting time. The advantages include a very delicate pin feel that is ideal for individually lifting BLT, a lower profile in the keyway and consequently more tool access, and ease in obtaining very light tension levels which are essential to BLT applied to various anti-pick cylinders.

I myself use a third kind of wrench. It has a rigid non-bending shank and a loose fitting working end. This tool is difficult to use initially, but it offers firm keyway placement, and an almost perfect one to one pin feel. Although most wrenches exert their force on the first quarter inch or so of plug, the American jam fit wrench with a long working end can be cut away or slimmed in width in the front while left regular in the back (the tip of the tool that goes farthest into the keyway).

This exerts no force at the front of the keyway, but rather a balanced force in the middle of the plug. Perhaps a better "feel". One style of wrench will be best for *your* technique, so experiment for the best results.

One other type of wrench that should be mentioned is the tweezer type with two very small working ends that bracket the

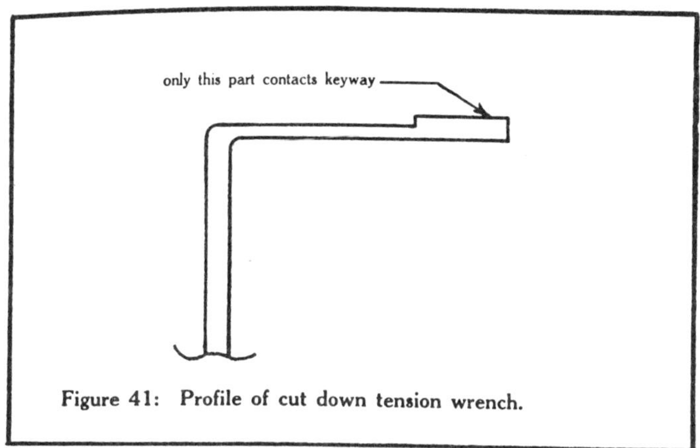

Figure 41: Profile of cut down tension wrench.

keyway and spread once in the lock, as shown in figure 42.

These are very good for limited access keyways, those that are too small for a regular wrench, and the double sided disc locks where each side must be individually picked. Their only disadvantages are that they tend to pop out of the keyway, which of course will ruin your day, and it is easy to hook your rake pick on one when raking a lock, with the same results. As

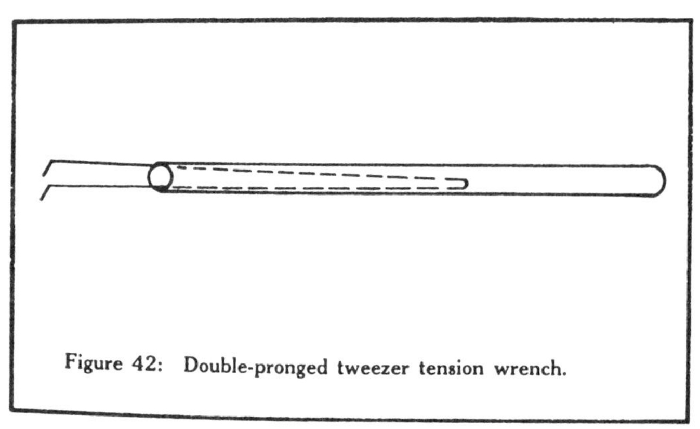

Figure 42: Double-pronged tweezer tension wrench.

always, directions for making your own are available in my book HOW TO MAKE YOUR OWN PROFESSIONAL LOCK TOOLS.

Now that we have all the theory and technique down for individually lifting BLT, let's quickly review and add a few practical suggestions. Select and insert a tension wrench, apply tension (unlocking direction) and insert the lifter pick, looking for the tightest bound and therefore fattest pin. Now without lifting the adjacent stacks with the tool shank, lift the tight pin untill it reaches the shear line. This arrival may be manifested as an increase or decrease in lifting pressure, the tension wrench may give a little, the plug may give a little, or there may even be an audible click. As always, do not overlift. When the pin has been picked, go on to the next fattest pin and so on. If you get all done and the plug will not rotate, rework through the stacks and see if a pin or two has not been fully lifted, or perhaps has slipped down. Also suspect the proper direction of rotation. A good indication that a pin stack has not been overlifted is that the bottom pin will fall back down loosely.

Just a word regarding lifter pick height selection. Ideally, you should select a pick that can be inserted without forcing any of the pin stacks up. Angling the pick in the keyway may help, see figure 43.

If this proves difficult, switch to a lower height pick (less distance between tip and shank) and lift the first pin, then switch to a regular height pick and again attempt to insert it. If it still won't go, revert back to the lower height and continue in this way until the regular height can be used. The higher the pick tip above the shank, the less chance of lifting an adjacent pin stack inadvertently with the tool shank.

I occasionally use a tool that has a barely perceptible diamond on the tip, like a miniature rake pick. I then rake the lock a couple of times to hopefully lift any high pins (requiring deep "V" cuts in the key) to their shear lines. This usually provides ample keyway access to proceed as usual then with lifting BLT. Remember that the maximum distance you will be moving a pin is rarely more that 1/16" and may be as little as .010". Also remember to adjust the tension if your pick is bending and not manipulating, as you are usually binding the pins too much. Above all, remember to keep track of where the shank of the tool is as well as the tip of the tool, since lifting adjacent pin stacks with the shank accidentally is very common. Try to keep the shank parallel to the wards in the lock, and well away from the other pin stacks. Another common habit is applying too much tension to the plug, and compensating for the increased bind by using the lifter like a pry bar, moving the operator end of the tool up and down, and levering the pin with the tip. This is wrong, and will surely lift adjacent pin stacks. Always move the tool up and down in parallel motion keeping it perpendicular to the lock face.

There are two methods that can be used to build up lifting BLT skills. One is well known, one is an Eddie original. The first teaching aid to use is to remove all of the pin tacks in a pin tumbler lock except one, and concentrate on locating and correctly lifting that one pin stack with a tool. Once this can be effectively done, another pin stack is added, and so on until all the pins are back in the lock. For this pin removal you will need a pin tumbler lock with key, a paper clip, and an ice cube tray. First, look for a plug retainer, something that prevents the plug from literally moving forward out of the cylinder when unlocked. It may be a cam at the tail of the plug, a metal clip riding in a groove cut in the plug, and covered by the same piece that covers the tops of the pin holes where the springs are. See figure 44.

Eventually you will find the retainer, and remove it. Next, insert the key, turn the plug about ten degrees off center, while keeping it still lined up within the cylinder. You may find that pressure to push the plug out the back of the cylinder will keep

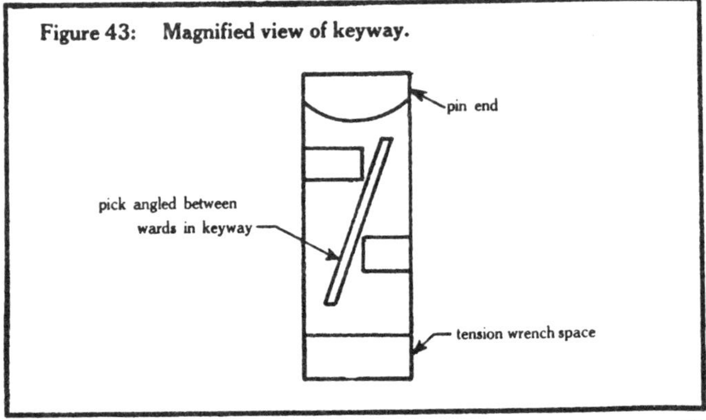
Figure 43: Magnified view of keyway.

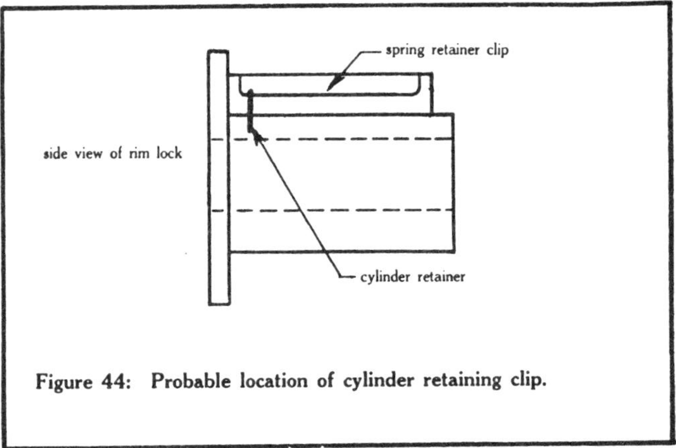

Figure 44: Probable location of cylinder retaining clip.

it lined up since most locks have a shoulder cut in the plug to act as a front plug retainer. In any event, the next step is to keep the plug off center about ten degrees, and, having the ice cube tray at hand, very slowly pull the plug out of the cylinder. At some point, a pin and possibly a spring will fall out of the inner cylinder hole being vacated by the plug. Watch for this, and tip the cylinder so as to drop these parts into one of the ice cube compartments. Slowly withdraw and remove the other pins and springs (the springs may not all come out, but don't worry) and put each in a separate compartment. Remember that a loose pin may become caught in the cylinder hole, so visually check to avoid mixing pins, and also keep the plug relatively upright because the bottom pins are just resting in the top of the plug, and should not be spilled.

Eventually, the plug and cylinder will be apart. Set the cylinder on the table, and place your finger over the tops of the pin holes and the pins in them. Now, uncovering each hole in turn, deposit the bottom pins in a separate compartment next to their corresponding top pins, finally unloading the plug. Remember which end is which. A cursory examination of the pins is now in order. The bottom pins should have chisel shaped ends which go down in the plug, and are wedged up by the key upon insertion. They will all be different lengths. The top pins also may be different lengths, but are usually all the same size, with two flat ends. Now insert the key in the empty plug, take the longest bottom pin you have, and insert it in different plug holes. Note how the wrong key/pin combination does not produce a shear line at the plug. Even if the bottom pins were scrambled in order, trial and error would eventually reorder them if the key was available for plug insertion. Also notice the usual shoulder at the front of the plug, and how it prevents direct shimming access to the pins and acts as a retainer.

Now, to reload the plug with one pin stack, first make sure all of the springs are removed from the cylinder. Next, select a pin stack, usually the third or middle set, and insert the bottom pin in the plug with key already inserted. Now fashion a set of tweezers from a paper clip, or buy a set, and insert the plug back into the cylinder. Now, with the plug end just up to the correct pin hole, thread the spring up into the hole, and then push the top pin into the hole also. Then push the plug in so that the plug covers the top pin and traps it. Remember through all of this operation to keep the plug turned the same ten degrees off center that you did during removal. The last step is to reattach the plug retainer and lock the cylinder. It is now ready for one-pin picking practice.

Additional pin stacks may be added using the previous techniques. One other technique that is useful is called shimming. Remember that the plug has a shoulder cut into the front to deny access, it is still possible to insert a thin strip of paper or metal into the back of the lock at the join between plug and cylinder. By manipulating each pin stack in turn with a lifter pick until the shear is reached, then inserting the shim between the pins, the lock can be opened. This is of course useful in a lock-out service, with no key available.

You learned to rake a lock in the disc tumbler section, but

the theory was omitted. As you know, if two billiard balls are lined up and a third strikes one of them, the force will be transmitted through one ball to the other ball, while the middle ball remains unmoved. This transfer of energy is just what occurs as a lock is raked. The wedging action of the pick jolts the bottom pin as it is withdrawn, and this force is transmitted to the top pin which jumps up. At some point, all of the top pins are airborne and the lock springs open. Note that the amount of tension on the plug must be very light to prevent binding the pins, and yet still quickly turn the cylinder once the shear line is established. Not only can the lowly rake pick impart force to the bottom pins, but there are snappers, (see figure 45) which

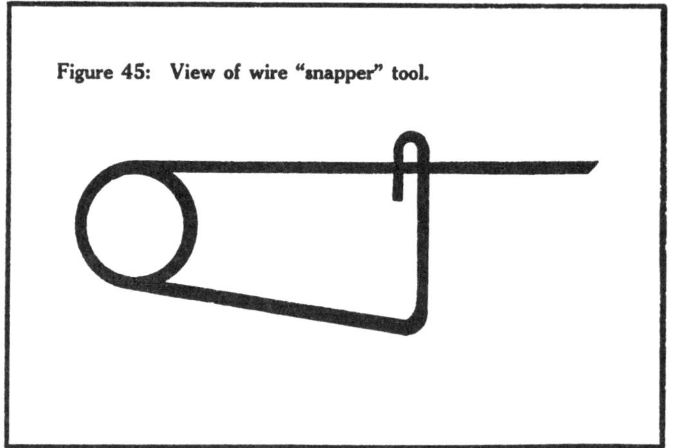

Figure 45: View of wire "snapper" tool.

are nothing more than giant safety pins with straight tools on the end to insert under the pins, and there are also pick guns that impart a snapping action to the same working end merely by pulling a trigger, as shown in figure 46.

Snapping a lock (same as raking) is quick and easy, where it works, and is usually tried before other BLT are attempted. There are two catches to snapping; (1) it either works well in 2-9 snaps or it doesn't work at all; and (2) it is easy to get addicted to it and ignore better skills development. Note that in disc tumblers, snapping is also effective even though there is no intermediate part. The special techniques section will cover snapping or vibration picking on the lever tumbler lock.

The principle of causing tumblers to line up by applying

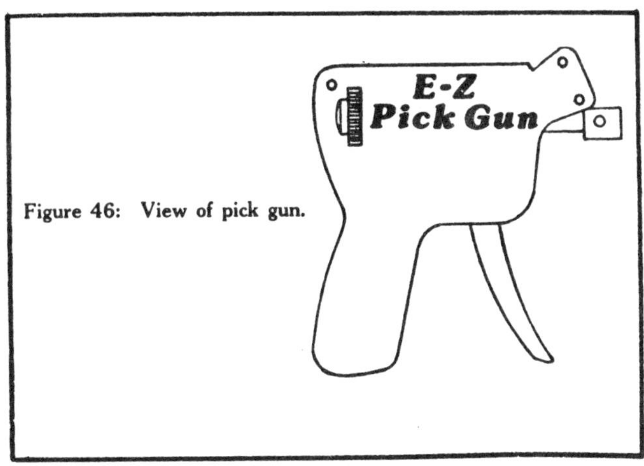

Figure 46: View of pick gun.

vibration to the lock has a few other applications. For instance, padlocks that have single beveled latches (just like on an exterior latch) that lock the shackle, can often be opened merely by applying a rapping force along the same axis that the latch travels to lock the shackle, and in the same or the opposite direction that you wish the latch to move.

The best way to apply these well directed blows is with a soft face hammer, or a plastic screwdriver handle. For unmounted pin tumbler lock cylinders, a rapping at the top or the bottom of the cylinder, again in line with the pins, will often effect an opening. Note that here you must apply some turning plug tension. Experts just grab a cylinder off center by its plug faces,

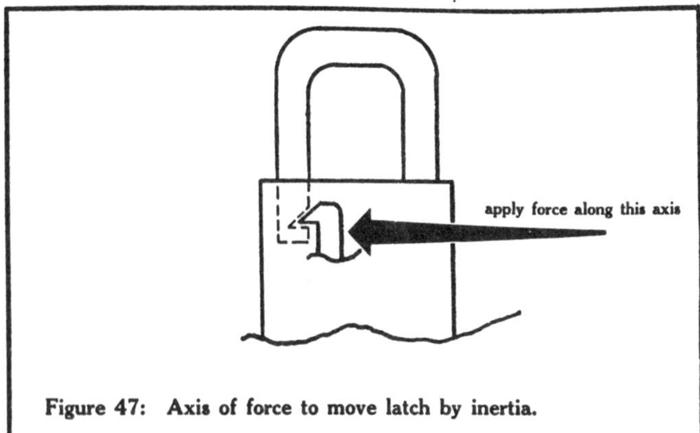

Figure 47: Axis of force to move latch by inertia.

and slap it against bench edges to open a cylinder.

Try to experiment with this technique, as it can be used to apply a moving force to any small part within a lock case, such as a lightly retained locking bolt. Magnetic locks that have no keyway may also be sometimes attacked by this method, if tension is exerted on the shackle. Most other references also mention electrically and battery operated vibrators like the pick gun. Some good adaptions of massage vibrators with straight tools on their moving parts have been done, and a clever person could attach a straight tool to the flexible part of a door buzzer, but the pick gun works just as well and is more portable. The soft hammer will also get you far.

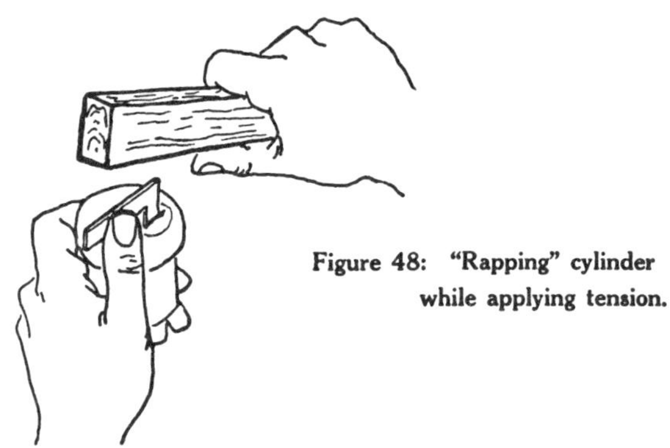

Figure 48: "Rapping" cylinder while applying tension.

CHAPTER 7

LOCK MODIFICATIONS TO THWART TAMPERING AND HOW TO OVERCOME THEM

This section deals with the modifications that lock designers make to thwart the gentle manipulation of the lock specialist. The battle between designer and specialist started in the 1800's and continues today. Usually, the better brands of lock (the top of the line) tend to incorporate anti-pick or anti-tamper devices, so eventually you will encounter all of the items listed here. This section has advanced information on how to identify and bypass these refinements.

The first topic is the Mushroom or spool tumbler. A typical type of this special pin tumbler is seen in figure 49.

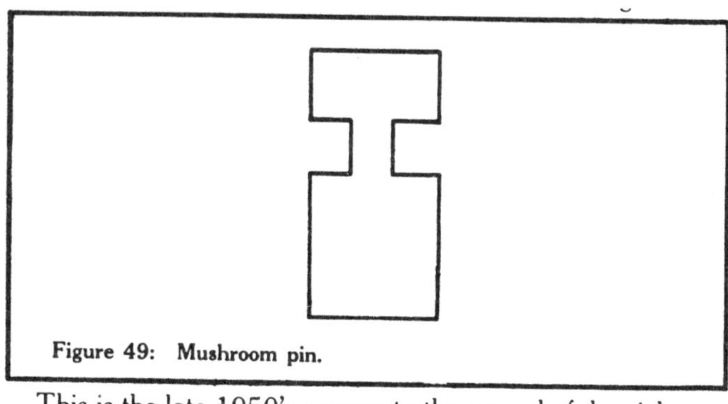
Figure 49: Mushroom pin.

This is the late 1950's answer to the spread of the pick gun. These top pins have grooves or ledges cut into their smooth sides that catch and jam on the shear line if the plug is put under tension, before the key elevates the pin to its shear. Therefore, if you are someday bypassing a pin tumbler lock and it suddenly unexplicably hangs up solidly, suspect a mushroom tumbler. To test for their presence, apply tension very lightly and attempt to raise each pin stack in turn. If one of the pin stacks when raised, causes the plug to rotate slightly in the opposite direction, that stack has a mushroom tumbler. These special pins were usually placed in positions three and five, with regular pins in the other stacks. This mixing was done so that the regular pins would fall back down and relock if tension were lessened in an attempt to clear the mushroom pins.

I interviewed a man who used to travel for CORBIN Lock Company (the first manufacturer that was generally associated with mushroom pins), and he said that it was common practice to make appointments for the sales talk, then show up early and open the house or office with a pick gun, making an easy sale. What the customer didn't know was that with a little extra knowledge, even mushroom manipulation is possible.

Let's see how. The first step is to identify the existence of a mushroom tumbler as per previous instructions. Try to eliminate other possible bypass problems like improper turning direction, and so on. Another good clue is the type of in-service application. Any commmercial exterior or limited access interior door, any medium to high security application may have a mushroom lock. Conversely, don't count on a mushroom lock in a low security or residential application.

Lock brand names like CORBIN, RUSSWIN, TUBELITE, KAWNEER may also be mushroom locks. I say *may* because a factory equipped lock may have the mushroom tumblers removed, and vice versa.

Once the problem has been identified, you can decide to attempt special BLT, or perhaps look for an easier lock or alternate means of bypass. Remember to follow the line of least resistence. The most reliable BLT for mushroom locks involves lifting all the pins with a straight tool up as far as they will go into the cylinder, then applying hard tension to bind them up in the lock. Next, apply light to moderate scrubbing with a rake or diamond pick while simultaneously and gradually releasing tension. If you have good technique at raking, the stacks will all slowly vibrate *down* to the shear line, not up like usual, and the pin stacks will reach their shear lines without involving the top mushroom pin. If you have bad luck, some of the regular pins will fall below the shear line, but these can be repicked in the conventional manner. If you have bad luck and lousy technique, some of the mushroom pins will fall down past the shear and you must start over again. Note in this technique pins are being manipulated in both directions. This concept of teasing a pin down if overlifted, can also be applied to regular locks -- for instance, if a tumbler is overlifted, merely scrub lightly and lessen tension slightly; but this is not foolproof.

Another BLT for mushroom locks is to proceed in the usual manner for individually lifting BLT, but apply very light tension so as to preclude catching a mushroom tumbler. As in the usual technique, the fattest pin must be lifted first. A good variation on this technique is to identify which stacks have the mushroom pins and over-lift those only, then scrub them down to the shear line, then lift the regular pins as usual. Perseverence is the rule here. Very vigorous raking or ripping of the lock will sometimes get the mushroom pins airborne as well as the regular ones, and the lock will open. Upside down picking (the first method discussed) with the snapper or the pick gun can also be highly effective. This is the method the sellers of mushroom locks don't like to talk about.

Disc locks also have their own form of the anti-pick device. In the disc lock, this takes the form of a tumbler with ends cut on an angle (figure 50) and matching bevels cut in the sides of the cylinder grooves.

In practice, a tumbler that binds against such a bevel when the specialist applies tension to the core, will tend to advance further into the cylinder groove and prevent effective picking. The test for this modification is to apply light tension to the plug and raise each tumbler in turn with a lifter pick. If the plug moves in the opposite direction of turning when the tumblers are manipulated, it has beveled end tumblers. As in mushroom tumbler locks, the technique of choice is some form of vibration or raking bypass, although very light turning tension applied during individually lifting BLT will also work.

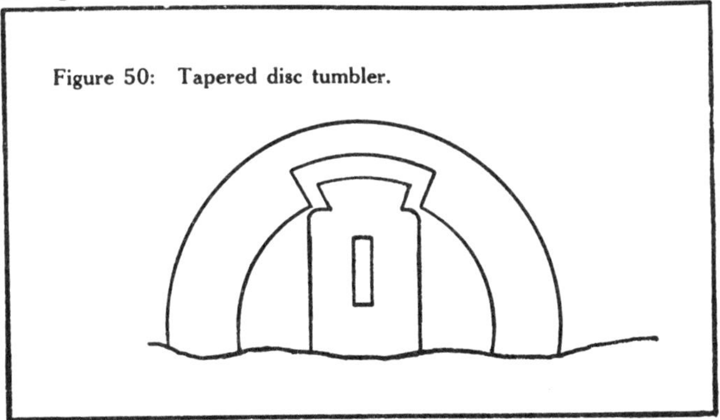

Figure 50: Tapered disc tumbler.

The lever lock also has its form of anti-pick device. Look at a diagram of the lever lock, paying close attention to the area on the lock where the stump meets the tumbler cutout surface. The modified locks have matching teeth or saw cuts on both the tumbler surfaces and the stump that mate whenever the stump is pressed against the tumbler.

Obviously, this prevents the tumbler from sliding freely against the stump and so makes bypass very difficult. As before, the counter to this is vibration picking, or very light tension during the picking process. A grating sensation as the tumbler is lifted is usually good proof that the anti-pick modification is present. Of the three, the saw-toothed stump/tumbler combination is the hardest to overcome, and you may want to try another part of the security chain instead.

Before we get into the topic of bypass of other parts of the locking mechanism, two more types of lock should be covered. The sidebar system is not really a lock type, but rather a part addition to wafer and pin tumbler locks. In figure 52 we have a normal disc tumbler lock in the locked position.

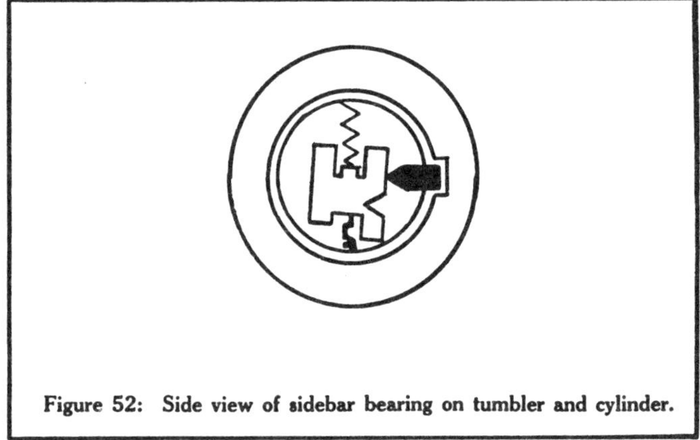

Figure 52: Side view of sidebar bearing on tumbler and cylinder.

The sidebar is the extra part whose square end protrudes into the cylinder notch located at 90 degrees to the regular tumbler notch, and whose other "V" shaped end rides against the sides of the tumblers. When the proper key is inserted, the "V" notches cut in the sides of the tumblers are all in line with the matching wedge end of the sidebar, and spring tension pushes the sidebar into the notches. This retracts the opposite end of the sidebar into the cylinder, and the plug is then free to

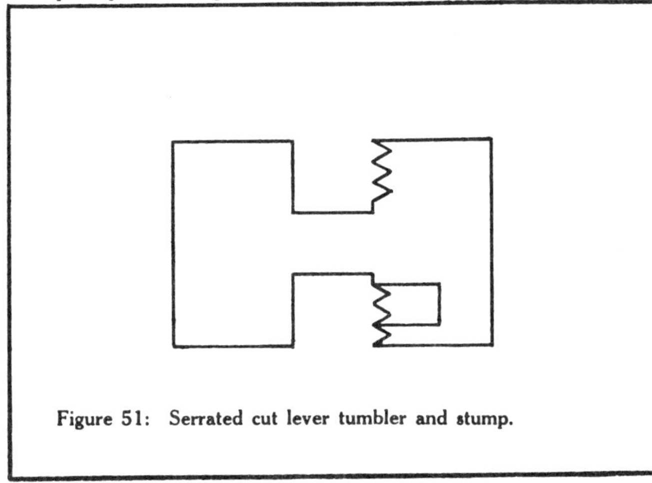

Figure 51: Serrated cut lever tumbler and stump.

turn. The subtlety of this system is that all of the tumblers must be lined up simultaneously, or the sidebar will not retract. If only one tumbler is too high or too low, it will block the sidebar from retracting.

The sidebar also prevents turning tension on the plug from binding the tumbler ends. This means that normal bypass methods will not work, since the tumblers cannot be bound and held in a picked position. There are alternative solutions. The sidebar does provide some feedback feel if all of the tumblers are almost perfectly aligned, so a pick that duplicates the key profile approximately will work the lock. These picks are called snake picks, (see figure 53) and come in two or three different profiles.

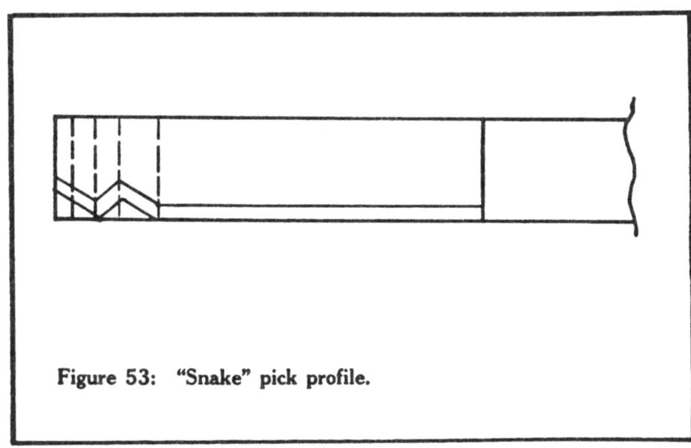

Figure 53: "Snake" pick profile.

Often, a length of piano wire can be field bent and modified to open a sidebar lock as well. When using these tools, move slowly, searching for the right angle of insertion, the right height of pick holding, and the right depth of insertion into the lock. If the feel is right but the lock will still not open, it means the profile is nearly correct, and very minor manipulation or bending alteration will do the job. It is wise to insert a tension wrench -- but apply no tension initially, wait until the feel is right. Note that excessive bending of a piano wire field pick may put the "V" bitting of the pick out of line with the discs or pins. The pick will of course still work if the pins or discs are not all bottomed out, but it is less stable that way. What profile is correct is really anyone's guess, but a good selection will be very helpful in adequately working these locks.

The most common form of disc sidebar is the GM automotive lock. Since this has a keyway shutter, inserting a tension wrench also is a good idea to permit unobstructed pick access. Some shutters hinge at one side, and others slide sideways. Examining a couple of such locks will show this. Pre 1968 - 1969 GM sidebar locks could be picked by individual lifting because of the fewer number of depths of cut that the lock had then. Locks built after this period can only be snake bypassed, or impressioned. These earlier locks also had, therefore, fewer possible key combinations, and try-out sets of keys cut to all possible combinations in half-depths were common and useful for medium-quick opening.

Modern locks are not so easy. Also, the comments applying to lock cleaning and lubrication prior to bypass apply to automotive locks in general, with a passion. Most of these locks do not work well with a key, so a clean, dry lock is mandatory to success. Pin tumbler sidebar locks are all very high security machines. In these locks each pin literally rotates on its axis left or right about 20 degrees, and brings a slot cut lengthways in the pin in line with matching projections cut on the sidebar. The chisel end of the bottom pin is then wedged left or right the precise angular distance by a key which is also cut on angles, and the lock's sidebar then retracts. The trick here is the key, cut with angular "V" cuts that the bottom pin's wedge shaped end rides in. The pin simultaneously rotates and lifts in this system.

The old adage "if it has a keyhole it can be picked", does not seem to apply to this lock type. MEDECO, a prominant manufacturer of these locks, has reportedly offered a money prize to the person who can bypass one of their locks. M.T.L., a friend of mine who usually doesn't require keys, has claimed that he bypassed a MEDECO cylinder once, and I have no doubt that he did, and that it can be done reasonably reliably, but the time involved would probably be prohibitive. The security chain probably offers a weaker link to attack.

As this goes to press, techniques and tools are becoming available for working sidebar locks. The working principle is to gain access to the sidebar by drilling through the lockface to it. Once any part of it is exposed, tension to push it into the plug (pushing it more tightly against the tumbler) makes bypass

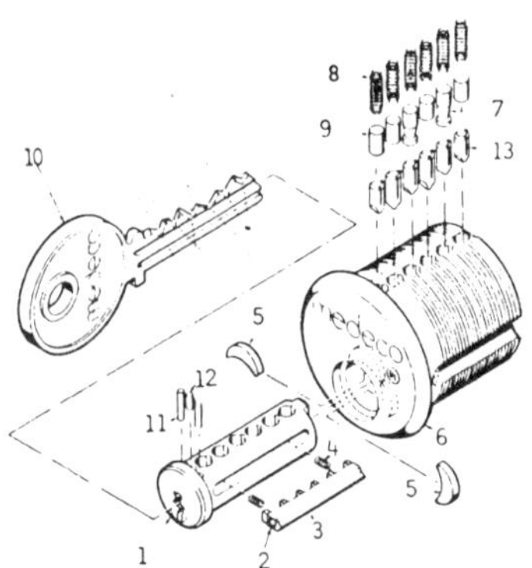

ASSEMBLY OF MORTISE CYLINDER		
ITEM	DESCRIPTION	REQ'D
1	Plug Mortise 6 Pin	1
2	Steel Ball (Hardened)	1
3	Fence 6 Pin	1
4	Spring Fence	2
5	Steel Insert (Hardened)	2
6	Shell Mortise 6 Pin	1
7	Mushroom Drivers	As req'd
8	Spring "Tumblers"	6
9	Driver (Hardened)	6
10	Key 6 Pin	1
11	Security Pin	2
12	Security Pin	1
13	Tumbler	6

Figure 54: Medeco sidebar lock diagram

possible. Drilling the GM automotive sidebar is easier that the MEDECO, since the latter has hardened steel inserts protecting pin wells, shearline, and sidebar. Angling the drill bit on a MEDECO may allow view to the sidebar. I strongly suggest you purchase a cylinder of this type and use it for practice. Once the sidebar is tensioned, the regular tools are used to manipulate the pin tumblers. Since this is a time-waster, try another part of the security chain. *Note* that except for the name MEDECO and perhaps EMHART, these locks have a keyway appearance identical to other pin tumbler locks.

CHAPTER 8
WAFER TUMBLER LOCKS

The last type of lock to consider is the wafer tumbler. This design was marketed by SCHLAGE to fill the gap between pin and disc tumbler security. It is in fact similar to the disc tumbler design, with parallel slots cut in the plug to accept seven wafers, and another parallel slot cut at the back of the plug to accept a special wafer type. There are two kinds of keyway and keys to fit each in this system.

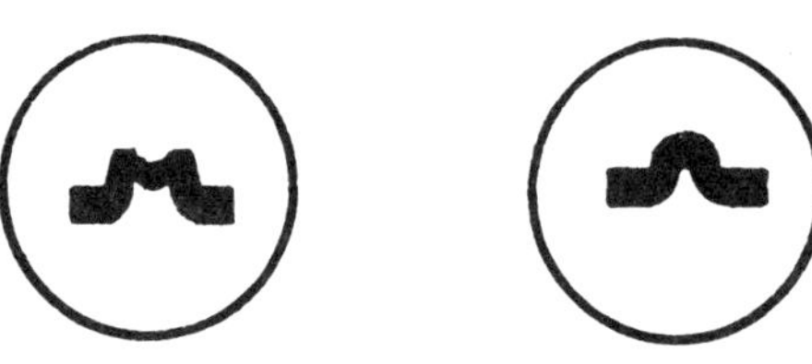

Figure 55: Keyway profiles for wafer tumbler lock.

The operation is simple. The rearmost wafer is called a master wafer, and it usually (in rest position with no key inserted) is protruded from the surface of the plug by spring pressure, just like conventional disc tumblers. The key must have no bitting at that point where it contacts the wafer if the key is to wedge the wafer and retract it into the plug. The next seven parallel slots are each filled with either a series (also no bitting on the key in order to retract them) or combination (requires a cut in the key at that point or else the key will wedge them out upon insertion and they will protrude from the plug surface) of wafers. See figure 56.

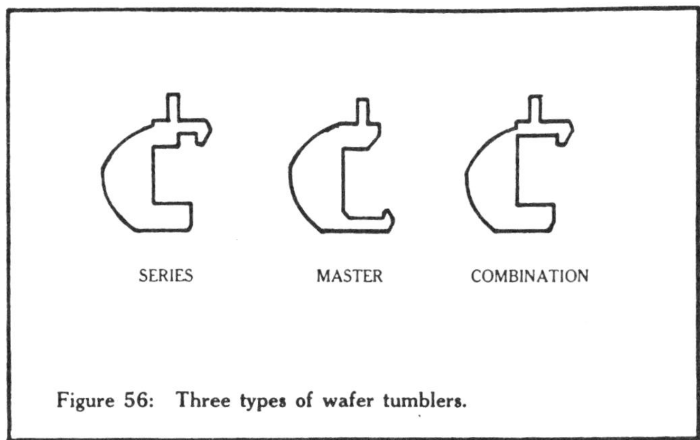

Figure 56: Three types of wafer tumblers.

By mixing the series and combination wafers in the slots, a variety of key combinations are possible. Remember though, the wafers only have one depth of protrusion, and the key only has one depth of bitting -- all or none. In addition, the extreme tip of the key acts on the one master wafer and retracts it upon insertion. The other side of the key tip is cut away to allow complete key insertion -- if the key is not cut away opposite the master wafer side, the key will not bottom in the lock, and the bitting and wafers will misalign. To ascertain which type of key you have, place it with the central "V" groove (the indented part) toward you, the tip to the left, bow to the right. If the key tip is cut away above the "V" groove, it is a "type one" key, if the tip below the "V" groove is cut away, if is a "type two" key. Observing which type will be of value in bypassing the lock

Identifying a wafer tumbler lock is very easy, due to the distinctive keyway, and the fact that most applications are SCHLAGE key in knob exterior locksets. There are two methods of bypass, one of them requiring specialized tools. The easy way is to insert a tension wrench to fit, use a lifter to count back to the eighth wafer, and retract it in toward the body of the plug. A fair amount of tension may be necessary to keep it retracted. The next move is to sort through all the wafers in turn with the lifter, finding the series wafers and manipulating them, and leaving the combination wafers alone since they are already retracted when at rest. The combination wafers will show slightly more resistance when moved.

The second method involves the use of a set of keys that have been cut down so that the tip retracts the master wafer, but the rest of the key is skeletonized so as not to operate any combination wafers. When this key is inserted and tension applied, then a separate straight tool is inserted in the portion of the key way left open by the key, and the series tumblers are retracted individually. This tool set is available from suppliers, or is described in my book HOW TO MAKE YOUR OWN PROFESSIONAL LOCK TOOLS, VOLUME 2.

One other method of bypass involves inserting the proper type key blank (1 or 2) into the lock, twisting hard, then maintaining tension and withdrawing the key almost all the way, then slacking off on the tension bit by bit until the combination wafers slip back into place. At that point, the plug should turn (theoretically), but this does not always work. Raking and other forms of vibration bypass do not apply here, to my knowledge.

One form of bypass this lock is particularly vulnerable to, is taking a quick impression of the key (wax or clay) or even a quick glance at the key, and cutting a duplicate, since keycut depth is not critical. The feel of bypass and the technique involved are really trivial, so don't spend too much time on these locks, but know them throughly. I am constantly amazed at the number of residential homes in the $50,000.00 range that are protected by these low-security locksets, but then they all have very kickable windows, too.

CHAPTER 9
BYPASSING LOCKS AND LOCKING MECHANISMS

This section covers various and different ways to bypass locks, locking mechanisms, and tips and tricks in general, including a brief discussion on a few forcible entry methods just for desperation situations.

Vibration picking for non-serrated stump/gate lever tumbler locks makes use of a piece of pick stock 9″ by a dimension not to exceed the height of the deepest tumbler cut on the key by .025 - .035. This tool must not move any of the tumblers when initially inserted under all of them, so adjust the width accordingly. To work it shake it up and down while simultaneously imparting a turning strain. If no results after thirty seconds, release tension and try again. This is of course not a fool-proof method.

As in combination locks, many lever locks have "windows" cut in the lock case at the point where the gate and stumps meet, allowing visual alignment of these parts. If you have a similar lock in your practice collection, or can open a lock next to the problem one (as in a bank safety-deposit box) measurements can be made, and a hole drilled through the door to line up with the window. Manipulation is then a snap with visual access.

Another bypass takes advantage of the fact that the stump of the lock is only riveted or spot welded to the bolt, and the application of heavy force to the bolt may well snap off the stump, permitting free bolt movement. The turning force can be applied directly with any hefty tool, but caution is advised because other lock parts may also break. The tool used must of course contact the bolt slot. A key blank cut down to size and inserted with a tool also inserted next to it in the keyway, may

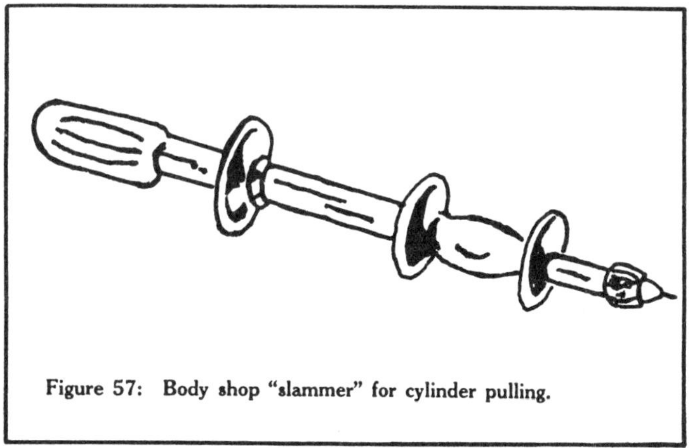

Figure 57: Body shop "slammer" for cylinder pulling.

provide the necessary force, the key moving the bolt, and the tool moving the key blank.

If you want to try professional methods, a nose-puller purchased from a supply house will do quite nicely for rapid lock removal. In a pinch, a large auto body dent puller or "slammer" with a sheet metal screw screwed into the keyway and then chucked into the slammer, may do the job.

Be sure to provide a proper support for the mounting surface if the lock is on a case or other small application.

One tip for those who think they have the levers almost manipulated using any of the preceding methods, but the levers are not exactly right in line. When this occurs, maintain tension and rap on the case with a soft-faced mallet to provide vibration. It sometimes works.

Brief mention was made of the detector lever lock that would have a special lever that immobilized or blocked all of the other tumblers' travel or the bolts' travel if the detector was overlifted. This rare construction can be overcome. The problem is to first locate the detector lever (usually at the back of the lock, but it can also be determined by feel), or by causing it to deliberately engage. It can then be disengaged by strong tension on the bolt in the locking or opposite direction. Once located, the other levers are picked first (individually lifted), and the detector is picked *last*. So much for lever locks.

One little trick occurs under disc tumble locks, and that involves the disc tumbler that does not want to bypass (very rare indeed). By selecting a suitable keyblank for the lock, inserting the tip and applying tension, and then lightly driving the key into the lock, the sharp edges of the discs are literally cut or worn away against the cylinder, which will make bypass very easy. As with all methods of force, though, it may actually lock you out permanently.

Continuing with alternate methods of bypass, let's cover the abuse of "T" handles. Many locking devices, particularly newer passage mortise locks and mobile home, camper cap, and screen door locks consist of either a "T" handle with plug inserted, or a "T" separate from the plug. Either of these two types may be attacked simply by exerting a strong turning force directly on the "T". The theory is that the "T" has more mechanical advantage than knobs or cylinder cams on the locking mechanism, and may literally break off the stops that prevent bolt movement. It may also be, however, that extreme pressure on the "T" will only damage the lock.

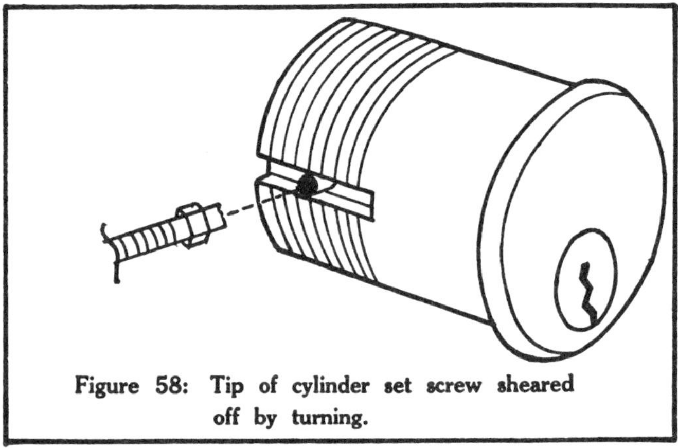

Figure 58: Tip of cylinder set screw sheared off by turning.

either by forcible turning or pulling. For mortise cylinder locks the method is to apply a strong pair of water pump or large adjustable-jaw pliers to the cylinder itself and turn it a quarter-turn so that the top turns toward the door edge. This action prevents breaking the lock itself, yet will shear off the end of the set screw that holds the cylinder in most locks from turning.

After the tip is sheared, the cylinder is rotated in whatever direction will unscrew it from the lock case, and the mechanism can then be directly operated with a screwdriver.

For rim lock cylinders, the turning action is even better in that since the lock turns, the cylinder connection bar may actually unlock the bolt when turned. If this is not the case, the cylinder must be repeatedly turned, even pried back and forth until it breaks loose from its holding screws. In some burglar-resistant locks, removing the rim cylinder allows a spring or gravity driven shutter to then drop down over the hole, denying lock mechanism access. Furthermore, the shutter and case often have matching teeth that prevent sliding the shutter back up. In this case, the shutter may be pulled forward and out of the locking teeth by a variety of methods, and then slid back. Sticky tape, prying on the end, many methods are possible.

Two very sharp-pointed awls can be used to move this security shutter. The first awl is driven sharply into the shutter at its bottom of travel. If the blow is sharp enough, the awl will stick in the shutter, allowing you to gently pull the shutter towards you and free of the locking teeth, then moved up. Now the second awl provides the next cycle of movement and so on till the shutter is completely open.

The final forcible method to consider is drilling a lock. The preferred course of action is to attempt to create a new shear line by drilling a hole whose axis comes exactly at right angles to the pin tumbler axis, and also the shear line where plug and cylinder meet. Remember that most cylinders have a shoulder cut at the front of the plug, so the actual shear line is not where plug and cylinder appear to meet.

Jigs that rely on pins inserted into the keyway are available to help guide a drill bit, but a little common sense in measuring will usually turn out correctly. The drill used should be variable speed and cordless. Some people have reported good luck with the BLACK and DECKER model. With all cordless drills, the rule is to use the battery pack frequently, or the ability to hold a

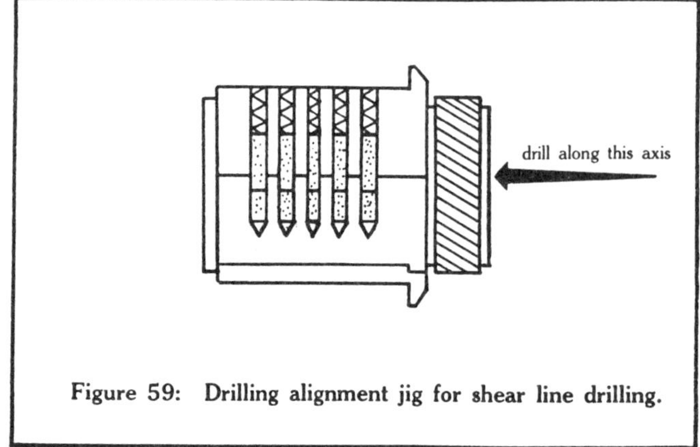

Figure 59: Drilling alignment jig for shear line drilling.

charge will be lost. An occasional complete discharge is actually good for the battery, but follow manufacturers' directions first. Any high-quality drill bit may be used, generally an 1/8″ high-speed steel machine twist bit.

When drilling for the shear line, the variable speed option is valuable for matching the "chatter" of the drill to the drill speed. Care should be taken when actually drilling through pin tumblers, because bits of chewed-up pin can get caught and jam the drill, causing breakage.

Besides drilling for a new shear, literally drilling away the entire plug a little at a time is also possible. For those locks that have plastic moulded plugs, this would be an ideal bypass. Drilling at an angle, avoiding the cylinder and trying for a lock mechanism is also possible, but only as a last resort. One point to mention here is that the high-security locks often have hardened inserts or free-rolling pins inserted at the most popular drilling points, just for you, the lock specialist. (See figure 54). If you encounter one of these, and are still committed to drilling, do the entire plug. Most drill jobs are only considered necessary when the lock mechanism fails in some way to operate, or normal keyway oriented bypass methods fail.

Shimming the latch bolt is covered in HOW TO MAKE YOUR OWN PROFESSIONAL LOCK TOOLS, VOLUME 1, as well as patterns for same, but since the credit-card shim entry became so very popular, lock manufacturers have added a dead-locking part to most medium security locks. This added mechanism prevents the bolt, whether beveled or dead bolt, from moving once locked if pressure is applied to the working end. The mechanism still provides for the latch being retracted by mechanism from the other end, namely the lock mechanism. In many cases of bypass the latch can be readily shimmed if the dead-locking function is first bypassed. In order to be able to manipulate the dead-locking mechanism, often some of the lock finish plate must be removed (the escutcheon). Even if the escutcheon cannot be completely removed, it may often be rotated around the cylinder, and then access is provided to manipulate and release the dead-locking lever. Once this is released, shimming may be accomplished on the latch itself.

Remember to have the shimming tool for the latch already in place, because the force or tension that released the dead-locking mechanism must be maintained throughout the latch shimming. If the escutcheon proves difficult to work around, sometimes the outer knob can be removed from the knob spindle simply by removing a set-screw. In other cases, the knob is retained by a pin which must be punched out. Often the door has such a loose fit to the jamb that the knob or door edge may be wedged far enough away from the jamb to release the dead-locking, and shimming may proceed as usual.

I have even seen doors that allowed the dead-locking latch to bottom in the latch pocket along side the latch, which made shimming a snap. The problem here was that the door could close too far. On panic bar locks, the dead-locking mechanism is often accessible by a shim inserted along side the thumb latch and lifted. Another way to release the dead-locking function only is to snake a wire around the jamb to the painic bar and hook and pull it just enough to release the dead lock. The latch can then be normally shimmed.

For all deadlocking mechanism, having a sample of the lock in general will provide good practice as well as tool design feedback, so try to expand your lock collection.

That's all! Good luck, and *practice!!*